THE WANN GAMBLER

BY

WARREN K. WASHBURN

2-10-12

Hi Doris

Hope you enjoy this book. and wishing you all the best, take care, maybe see you sometime.

Sincerely

Warren Washburn

Note:

In order to protect the privacy of certain individuals who appear in this book, names and other identifying characteristics have been changed. Also, I remember the substance of all these events but maybe not all the details. However, the truth remains substantially intact. ww

CHAPTER ONE

Monday night football, late in the fourth quarter. Wanting my Eagles to run up the score on the Cowboys. The phone rings. This late, has to be a wrong number. I let it ring twice more. I pick up.

"Warren, they're taking your dad to the Lincoln hospital."

"Who's they?"

"He made me call an ambulance."

"What's wrong?"

"Has lots of pain in chest and stomach. You better come. Bryan Memorial."

"Have to get off work, Mom. Try to be there early tomorrow morning."

The next day I drive two hours to the hospital, walk into his room.

Mom is reading a magazine and snapping chewing gum. I wonder how she gets away with that. He used to blame her gum snapping for throwing off his concentration. It jinxed him, he said. Mickey is reading a newspaper. Dad is sitting up, an IV stuck in his hand.

He moans, "Warren, you won't believe what they put me through."

"Have they found out anything?"

"Kidney stone or gallbladder problem," Mom says.

Dad pushes against his right side. "Mickey, go get the racing form."

Mickey leaves, nurses walk in and out.

Dad barks at them. "Where the hell's my phone? I ordered one last night. Damn betcha it'll be on my bill."

"Warren, go with 'em. Get the phone and hook it up."

I shrug my shoulders and walk out. *Why hurry*, I think. *I can't be around him more than five minutes before he starts ordering me around.*

Ten minutes later I hook up his phone. Mickey and Dad study the entries for the Ak-Sar-Ben races in Omaha.

Dad moans again. "Damn this place. Where the hell's the doctor?"

He shifts his large frame around, groaning and cussing. He gives Mom his bookie's phone number. Tells her to dial it.

Mickey nods his head toward the door. I follow him.

"Did you hear about last night?" He asked.

"Just that he had an ambulance drive him here."

Mickey laughs. "I was there. They brought in a stretcher. He laid down on it. They couldn't lift him. He walked out to the ambulance and laid down. The guys came back to town. Told everyone about it at the pool hall."

"Anyway," I say, "I don't think it's serious if all he's going to do is lay there and bet the ponies."

"Nah, think he'll be home tonight."

I walk back into his room. Dad hangs up the phone. Mom is back in her chair.

"Mickey, who you like in the fifth?" Dad asks. "Think Nellie Q's ready to go?"

"Mom, I need to get back to work," I said. "Dad, I think you're getting better. Probably be home tonight. I'll keep in touch."

Both tell me goodbye. As I walk out the door, I hear Dad say, "Mickey, spot me twenty. I'll hit a lick this afternoon and pay you back."

WANN, NEBRASKA

In John Steinbeck's Cannery Row, the poetic introduction of Monterey is this: "It is a poem, a stink, a grating noise, a quality of light, a tone, a habit, a nostalgia, a dream."

What can be said creative about Wann, Nebraska? It's not on the map and hasn't been for years. But it still exists. I could give anyone a five minute tour of Wann. I could point out the structures that still exist which seemed so large to me during the 1940s.

You couldn't call Wann a town or village; there wasn't enough substance. Doesn't the word "village" bring to mind quaintness--a white church spire, red and yellow leaves, and whitewashed dwellings?

Wann was a Podunk, a stopover, a whistle stop. To some misguided fools, Wann was a laughter—like "Wann, two, three." During the late 1880s, a few dwellings materialized on the level Platte valley after Wann was named for a railroad stop. In the years that followed, a church, a school, a general store, a bank, and a grain elevator began to operate.

Don't be fooled by the smallness of Wann. Our Washburn clan kept the Podunk alive with strawberry picking, sweet corn husking, tomato planting, game playing, joke telling, and the raising of chickens, hogs, and cows. Even Aunt Jemima once visited Wann.

If you lived near Ashland or Wann (both located near the Platte River in eastern Nebraska) you probably knew of my Dad, Harry S. Washburn. He wasn't one of those two-bit gamblers who would put a fiver on the Bears or send their two-dollar Daily Double bet to the Aksarben racetrack. Or the ones who played nickel/dime pitch or poker games in the Ashland Legion Club or the Memphis pool hall.

Gambling was Dad's choice of lifestyles, his way of supporting a family of seven. If Ashland had a gambling business, he would have been the president and majority stockholder.

He taught his four sons to read by using the past performance sections in the Daily Racing Form. He taught us lineage by showing that the race horse Irish Bull was out of Irish Delight and Spotted Bull. When he took us to the races, he found empty Cracker Jacks boxes for us to fill with discarded tickets. That night we practiced bookkeeping skills. Each ticket checked against the program he had marked with the win, place, and show horses.

When we were old enough, he educated us in the skill of playing poker. Never draw to an inside straight, keep a poker face and know the odds based on the face-up cards. At times, he would be gone for weeks, especially in the winter. He drove to Hot Springs, Arkansas or the Hialeah racetrack in Florida.

Consequently, our family life was like a roller coaster ride. When he won, we would eat all the candy we wanted, see picture shows, drink soda pop, and jingle coins in our pockets. When he lost, we kept our mouths shut, went hungry, and lived in houses with no indoor plumbing.

If Dad were alive, I couldn't tell this story. Oh, not for the usual reasons one might expect. Like he might complain that it's a bunch of lies, and I've got it all wrong and what the hell am I doing revealing our family's life, making him look awful.

He would take over. He would write how the family he grew up in with nine children survived the Depression on a small farm. How he rode the rails to Kansas City looking for work in exchange for a meal. How he joined the Civilian Conservation Corp. and sent his earnings to his mom. How his gold watch was stolen at gunpoint at the Hialeah racetrack.

That's what would happen. I can remember fifty episodes from our family's life during the time when I was five years old to fifteen.

But him? He could tell a hundred and fifty. That's why the story couldn't be told. Barnes & Noble doesn't own enough shelves to hold all the books.

I'm not afraid of him now as I used to be. I suspect that if he read this story, he would enjoy most of it. He might correct me on a few incidents. Nonetheless, I will tell the tale from a good memory. I never spent time trying to understand why I didn't become a gambler. Probably I didn't possess the right stuff; maybe it was because of my rebellion.

Apparently, Dad never realized the extent of my longing to escape from his lifestyle. I kept my desire hidden because I was too young, too scared and too gutless.

July 29, 1941 entry in Mom's diary. The day of my birth, same as my Dad's birthday.

"Oh dear God, I've just found out my baby has a crippled foot. I love him so much, why did this have to happen."

CHAPTER TWO

Many untamed things sprouted in Wann in the 1940s—Hollyhocks, bitter gooseberries, fuzzy peaches, yellow dandelions, sticky thistles, swift snakes—but just as wild were the four Washburn boys. In birth order—Norman H., Warren K., Clark M. (Mickey), Kenneth A.

We caused our mother (Violet N. Russell Washburn) lots of grief, but she never gave up on us.

June, 1989

"I can't take care of your dad anymore. Can you move him to a home?"

Mom phoned on a Monday. To move, to place, to force him into, it's all the same tune. I'd rather not do it. If he raises a stink, I'm not sure how I'll handle him. I'll try for Mom's sake.

I thought about how his life had come to this point. He probably knows this move will be final. The last time I visited he walked out of his bedroom pushing a walker. He began to cry. He couldn't stand having one of his sons see him helpless.

When we were young, he traveled to horse races. Then he would appear, we adjusted to his heavy-handed routine, and days later he'd be gone. When I became a teenager, I was glad when he wasn't home. Life was easier and more fun.

Sleeping that night was tough. Flooding my thoughts were memories of our family life. Our first home was a four-room clapboard shack. Later we moved to a small brick building which had electricity. Neither had indoor plumbing. My first memory was of a scary night when Dad wasn't home. The year was 1949, and we were living in the brick building.

1949

I was eight years old and knew that we were poor. However, my brothers and I accepted what we were born into.

Sour green apples filled our bellies. Mulberries and raw turnips were tasty. A sliced radish on bread was my favorite. Sometimes

Grandma Washburn gave us an item from the general store. The best treat was a fudgsicle. We stayed alive and appreciated the smallest toy.

When Dad was gone, life was calmer, but we tended to get out of control. More than once Mom made us promise to stop cussing. When we hung around with other boys everyone cussed. It was fun to cuss. Dad was an expert. Sometimes Mom cried, and then she would walk over to the school grounds and sit. Usually that settled us down for a few days.

There were many nights when I wished for Dad's presence. Like the night of my snake dream.

I dreamed that snakes were chasing me. There were thick bull snakes, fast blue racers, green and black garter snakes. I wanted to freeze, hoped they wouldn't see me. My mouth felt dry. I couldn't breathe. My legs cramped and stopped moving. I wanted to reach the cement slab in front of our brick house; then I would be home free, time out, safe.

I woke with a start. When I realized my fear came from a dream, the cobwebs cleared from my head. I heard a low rumble of thunder a mile away by the Platte River. But I knew that wasn't what woke me. I could feel dampness on my chest and arms. My legs felt weak and covered with goose bumps.

I was scared of many things, but I learned that horrible dreams faded in the light of day. Besides, I realized what caused the dream. My brothers and I had killed a snake the day before.

"Come on guys, a snake!"

Norman jumped in the ditch which was across the sandy road in front of our house. He raised a branch and smashed it down. Mickey, Kenny and I ran across the road. We grabbed cottonwood branches. I spied the large bull snake trying to escape into a hole underneath the cottonwood tree which grew out of the ditch.

"Head him off, head him off!" Norman cried as weeds, leaves, and dust flew up from our strikes.

It bothered me to watch living animals die, but I couldn't stand by and let my brother down. Mick and Ken joined the battle without fear, smashing their sticks onto the snake that was fighting for its life.

"Get him, get him!" Norman yelled.

The bull snake twisted around. We smacked his head and any part of his long body we could reach. All the while we stayed away from his mouth. Fear and excitement charged me as I took a turn. I was glad when my club broke. I backed out of the way. Seeing the smashed body and the faint red of blood on the snake's slimy-looking skin made me sick to my gut. Soon, the only thing moving was the snake's twitching tail.

"Push him out to the road," Norman commanded, "but watch out, he may be faking it."

We used branches to push the snake to the edge of the road and then stretched him out.

"Let's get a yardstick to measure him," Norman said.

"Why you boys always killing things?"

We looked up and there stood Grandpa Washburn leaning on his hoe. He wore a railroad man's dusty grey hat. Bib overalls covered his long-sleeved, sweat-stained blue shirt. His wrist bones hung down from his shirt sleeves. His fingers appeared knotted at the joints, and his nails were black.

He was right. For unknown reasons, we killed most wild animals on sight, or tried to. Snakes, toads, grasshoppers, sparrows, blackbirds, mice and rats. It seemed as if it were our duty.

Grandpa blew out a puff of smoke from his cigarette. He had a way of holding it that made it hard to see.

I looked at the beat-up body of the snake. Fear and excitement vanished, replaced with a sick feeling. Norman was Grandpa's favorite grandson, but even he didn't say a word.

"Don't you boys know that bull snakes eat mice and rats? Those varmints are in the sheds behind your house."

"Thought he was going to bite me," Norman spoke, but not with confidence.

"You boys straighten up. I need you two oldest hoeing tomatoes by seven in the morning. Wear your brogans."

Grandpa turned and walked down the road toward his house.

"Norman, what's brogans?" I asked.

"He means our clodhoppers."

We watched him until he turned back and said, "Getting a television set this Saturday. I want you boys to come over and watch rassling with us."

As we looked down at the dead snake, the summer sun began to settle in a red haze of dust. We gave the snake a few kicks with our clodhoppers, just to make sure. Then from our house we heard Mom's call.

"Supper time."

We threw our branches down, and then walked across the junk-filled cement slab in front of our building. We entered our main room which served as an eating-place and a bedroom. Our plates sat on the table with a mound of mashed potatoes on each.

"Mom," I said, "Grandpa says they're getting a TV this Saturday. Can we go watch it?"

"We'll see."

"What we having for supper?" Norman asked.

Mom spooned a helping of tomatoes and hamburger onto our potatoes. She said, "goulash."

One glance and I was up and running outside, holding my mouth. The tomato sauce and the meat looked like the smashed body of the snake. I upchucked off the cement slab. I couldn't eat anything so went to bed with slight hunger pangs.

The fright of the snake came back in the nightmare. I lay awake waiting for my heart to stop pounding. I was afraid of many things: My Dad's temper, getting outran by any girl at school, and the Arkansas Shultz boys who would beat me up if Norman wasn't near.

Fear grew in my mind. I never believed in imaginary monsters, but I sensed something was wrong. I stayed awake on my half of the couch; Norman slept on the other half.

Our home had two regular beds. Mom slept in one and Mick and Ken in the other. The couch Norman and I slept on was in the main room. I glanced at the dim light bulb hanging at the top of a box of twenty-five baby chickens. I didn't hear a peep.

The light was not what scared me. Even the foul smell from the chicken droppings on the box bottom wouldn't wake me. I grew up with that smell. No, there was something else. Something alive, a new fear.

Wann didn't maintain streetlights. When evening came, darkness settled around the houses. I turned toward our large front window which had no curtain. It had shades, but they stuck bunched up at the top, ripped and broken. I saw a swaying cottonwood branch.

Then, not believing my eyes, I watched a shape move. I began to breathe harder.

I saw the outline of a man's hat moving sideways. I thought my heart might pound out of my chest. The hat stopped moving and then faded from view. How I wished that Dad was home. I tried to speak out, but only a croaking sound came forth.

Norman stirred next to me. My heart thumped. I forced my eyes away and then back to the window. Nothing but a few branches. Then again, a shape appeared in the window. I froze. The head and hat stopped as if someone were staring straight at me. The hat looked like what a hobo would wear.

The thought of a bum reminded me of what happened at noon. We were sitting on our worn-smooth wooden chairs waiting to eat. Mom walked out from the vault-size kitchen and said, "All we have is one hotdog apiece."

There were no complaints. We knew better than to ask for dessert.

"Here you go."

She placed a slice of white bread on our plates. Then she forked out one boiled wiener for each. The smell of boiled hotdog water almost made me gag.

"If you're still hungry, pull radishes out of the garden. This afternoon we'll walk by old man Larson's farm. Look for apples in the ditch."

She looked around to see if anyone had a better idea. Then she said, "Drink a glass of water with your hotdog."

We heard the screen door creak and a low knock on the door. Had to be a stranger, our relatives usually walked right in. I looked at Norman and Mom. The slight look of fear in their eyes caused my gut to tighten. Our eyes focused on the door as Mom opened it. She blocked the hobo from looking in, protecting her brood with her body.

We heard a mumble and then Mom closed the door. She picked up a piece of newspaper, placed her hotdog on it and wrapped the paper around it. She handed out her care package.

She said, "I'll bet he'll be surprised to find a warm sandwich."

Mickey asked, "Mom, what will you eat?"

She walked to the kitchen and then came back munching on a

saltine cracker.

I stood up and peeked out the window. The hobo walked toward the Wann General Store and the railroad tracks. He was bundled in rags, wearing a strange hat pulled down over his ears. He didn't glance at the dead snake.

Going back to lunch, I said, "Maybe he's a gandy dancer."

"A hobo," Norman stated.

"A bum," Ken blurted out.

The hobo is back looking in, I thought. Again the shape moved sideways and disappeared. I felt I might pee in my shorts. When the screen door made a creaking sound, I thought about our dog, Jigger. He usually slept near the door. He was a heavy sleeper even through thunderstorms. I slid off the couch and crawled past the table toward Jigger. I thought if I could wake him, he might hear the hobo and start barking.

I knew I couldn't stop anyone. The Shultz boys said my arms looked like toothpicks. Ilene Nitz said I looked like Ickabod.

I saw Jigger's closed eyes. His paws danced a twitch. I heard a muffled sound at the door. I looked up as the door handle turned and then stopped. I reached out to shake Jigger, but a hand grabbed my arm. I froze.

"What are you doing?" Mom whispered.

"Sshhh. There's someone outside."

"Nonsense, you're probably imagining it. Maybe you heard Jigger bump against the door."

Jigger sat up and began to scratch his head. He paid no attention to any outside noise.

"Mom, I saw someone in the window and heard the screen door open."

We moved to the window and looked out.

"There." I pointed to a shadow moving by the cottonwood tree.

"I see it," Mom said, "now go back to bed. The door's locked. I'm going to sit up by Jigger for a while."

I climbed back on the couch and then peeked at the back of the house. I saw my younger brothers on their bed. Above them was also a large window. A shadow moved, but it was a tree branch. When my heart slowed down, I drifted off to a troubled sleep. The dream and the terror had given me a headache. *That chicken poop smell is getting worse*, I thought.

The next morning I ran to Mom.

"Mom, Norman doesn't believe me that the hobo looked in our window last night."

"Now stop that kind of talk. You probably saw a tree branch."

That's fine, I thought, *but I'm going to get Jigger to sleep beside me tonight.*

Before school, we sat down to a breakfast of mushy oatmeal.

"We're out of milk," Mom told us. "I put a small piece of butter on your oatmeal. Sprinkle a little sugar on it and stir it up."

After breakfast, I walked over to the tree. I looked at the remainder of the bull snake, covered with ants and sand. I walked near it and then looked carefully at the tree. I saw nothing. Still scared, I walked one block to the Wann Elementary School for lessons and recess.

That afternoon I started to walk home until I saw Dad's black Chevy sitting out front. I broke into a gallop until a reminder brought me up short. If he had won at the races, we were in for treats. Maybe a bag of store-bought cookies or a ten-cent toy. But, if he had rotten luck, no one would dare ask for a nickel for a soda pop or a Hersey candy bar.

When I walked in he was bending over the chicken box. He took one look at me.

"Get the hell over here and look at this."

Oh-oh, I thought, *now I'm going to catch it.*

"Why the hell the papers aren't clean at the bottom?"

The feeling of guilt gripped me. I kept my eyes down. "Guess I forgot this morning."

"Dammit, clean this mess now. Look at the waterer. Look empty to you? And look at the chicken shit in it. What the hell good does it do me to spend money on chickens when you can't even do a simple job?"

I knew when it was best to keep my mouth shut.

"You're lucky I don't take the yardstick to you."

"Quit being so hard on him," Mom said. "He's been sick."

"Yeah, well what was it this time? Hope you didn't take him to the doctor. I can't pay bills or buy medicine."

"He had the mumps, but got over them. Stayed home a week from school."

That word "mumps" made my jaw glands ache. Mom had cured me by mentioning the possibility of a hot water enema.

We kept our eyes down during supper so as not to raise his wrath. Boiled bologna and sauerkraut was on the menu. Dad didn't like it. I figured he was broke, no "happy days are here again" for us boys. I forced a piece of bologna and sauerkraut down, and then I snuck my bologna to Jigger.

Dad looked at Norman before supper ended.

"Heard you had to stay after school. What for this time?"

"Just a little fight at recess with Nathan Shultz."

I knew that was a lie, but I kept quiet. At noon he and another boy had tried to raise a girl's dress. She told on them.

Dad grabbed the yardstick. "Get out in the kitchen."

We heard the five whips. Norman came back with misty eyes, but he wouldn't cry. I wished I was as tough as he was. Mom sat with her head in her hands. Whenever I was whipped, I began to cry on the first strike, trying to gain sympathy.

Going to bed again with an uneasy stomach, at least I felt safe. Nothing to be frightened of tonight. No snakes, no hobos, I wouldn't look at the window. The chicken box was clean, no bad odor. With Dad staying here, I planned to sleep soundly.

I caught talk coming from the kitchen.

"Staying for a while this time I hope."

"Yeah, I'm quitting those damn races. Maybe get a job."

"Guess I've heard that before."

I heard Dad cuss but just then Norman nudged me with his elbow.

He whispered, "Remember Grandpa telling us that where there is one snake there has to be two? Let's dig at that hole in the ditch tomorrow. Maybe we can kill another one."

I was silent for a few seconds before saying, "Okay."

I hoped that tomorrow he would forget about it and that other activities would occupy our time. All I wanted was a decent night's sleep and a normal family life.

CHAPTER THREE

June, 1989

    I leave early for the two-hour drive to Lincoln to move Dad. Memories of a family ruled by the gods of luck and chance overflow my mind. Driving slowly on the interstate, I want to delay the inevitable.
    I think that Wann's population in the 1940s was about thirty. Everyone raised chickens; Dad assigned us boys to take care of his pigs and calves.
    The worst shack in Wann was our first home. No electricity, lighting by kerosene lamps; no indoor plumbing, used the wooden outhouse. There was a sink pump. A pot-bellied stove heated the rooms. Dad burned pieces of wood, coal, or corn cobs. Once he filled the stove with dry field corn.
    I think about Dad. He was well-suited for the impulse life. He was in his teens when he began going to the horse races with his dad. The obsession hooked him. It flourished unnoticed like a deadly disease until too late. The four racetracks in Nebraska spaced their seasons so that he was never without his daily fix except for winter.
    He was smart enough to handle people to his own liking. He recovered from losing streaks by doubling back his bets. He was something else when he was winning. Cracked jokes, laughed, tossed coins to his boys as people throw popcorn to pigeons. We were country-smart enough to eat up during those times.
    Dad was at his best then. He invited his brothers and sisters. Cheap Mogan David wine and Papst Blue Ribbon beer appeared. When he told jokes we all laughed.
    My brothers and I acted giddy, jumped around, mouthed off. Who cared about the future? Maybe we would go hungry next week. Maybe we wouldn't mind that our shanty had no indoor plumbing. Dad was in his element. All was right with the world.
    His favorite sayings were, "I'm on a roll" and "I'll hit a lick." Once he borrowed half the money I'd saved to go to college. He promised, "I'll hit a lick next week and pay you back." Yeah right, like there's a tooth fairy and Santa Claus. And Wann will be the capitol of Nebraska some day.

I stop in front of their rent-subsidized apartment in Lincoln. I sit for a few minutes to build myself up for what I have to do.

Memories of life in Wann invade: Going with Dad to the horse races, cherishing the one Christmas present, rounding up escaped hogs, begging grandparents for food, nearly burning down the church building, being baptized in a sandpit, attending the Wann elementary school and the Christian Church.

1946-47

I remember living in the shanty when I was five and six years old. Norman was thirteen months older. Mick and Ken were two and one years old. My earliest recollection of Dad was when he scared me, so it stuck in my memory.

For Norman and me, the exploration of Wann was never ending. We studied the immediate life in puddles after a rain. We climbed high in cottonwood trees. We ran races on the roads. We would climb under a barbed-wire fence and scout out the sandpits. We would sneak inside a forbidden door to the elevator to gawk at the wooden gears covered with corn dust.

Talk of war and hatred of Japs and Germans dominated life. Dad's history of the early '40s was unclear. He wasn't in the war since he didn't pass the physical. He worked in Canada and Alaska for a construction company which built a highway for the army.

One afternoon his younger brothers appeared with their spades.

Dad ordered, "Norman and Warren. Get your jackets on. Get outside and do some work."

I didn't want to. It was chilly, and I felt sick.

When I walked out the back door, I sulked, my head down. One of my clodhoppers kicked a glass waterer. It tumbled sideways and glass scattered. I must have looked stupid, staring at the damage. Dad grabbed my arm and yanked me toward him. I felt the sting of his hand on my butt.

"Watch where you're going. And quit your damn pouting or I'll give you something to pout about."

Mom never yanked me around. I didn't cry or blame Dad. I thought it was my fault. After the swat, I glanced at Norman who had picked up his toy shovel. He was a worker. We were skinny, not the image of healthy American youths.

I had a bloated belly due to poor eating habits. I was as sick looking as a Nebraska weed in the boiling summer heat. Yet we did not have that bland look of dumbness either. We accepted our life style until our eyes were open to the fact that other families were so much better off.

To me, any family that had indoor plumbing and an upstairs was rich folk. I wondered what it would be like living upstairs, that far from the ground. I worried I would become dizzy and drop out if I were ever upstairs in a house.

Our two uncles, Wendell and Larry, were shorter than Dad. He was large-boned, like his mom. The uncles appeared wiry and strong, like Grandpa Sam. Wendell smoked a cigarette. They wore sweat-stained baseball caps, jeans, and red flannel shirts. Dad pointed toward the outhouse.

The wooden outhouse sat in the middle of a weed patch. A cob pile was close by. Between the outhouse and the cob pile were leftovers of a makeshift chicken pen.

Dad said the outhouse wasn't worth a tinker's damn. The uncovered cobs molded from the fall rains. There could be a use for the chicken items if Dad bought baby chicks. He walked over to me.

"Find a pail. Fill it with cobs. Learn to do some work."

How I wished I was with Mom. I glanced at the shack, hoping to see her. Our shack sat between the outhouse and a sandy road. All roads in Wann had loose sand covering them. The neighbor across the road, old man Vosler, liked to tell how he used to raise chickens in our shack.

The shack was made of narrow clapboard, charcoal colored. The door was white pine. A window appeared on each side of the door. Covering the top half of the windows were tan shades with rips. Old towels covered the bottom half. Inside the shack were four rooms separated by slats that had chunks of grey plaster between them. If a piece of plaster appeared loose, Norman and I would pry it out and throw it away.

I picked up a grey pail and sat down on the cob pile. I grabbed a cob and tossed it toward the pail. If it missed, I didn't care. I stopped to watch the men pace off a certain distance from the outhouse. They began to dig a rectangular hole.

The Platte Valley soil was dark and easily removed. The three men worked well together. The Washburn clan learned to face disasters by joking and teasing until someone became pissed off.

Dad asked, "You guys drinking any beer? Puts lead in your pencil."

Wendell answered, "Ain't doing me no good. Got no one to write to."

They laughed, but I didn't see anything funny.

"Did you hear the one about the lady sitting on the stool in the filling station?" Larry asked.

I heard him tell the story, and they laughed again. It didn't make sense to me, so I began throwing more cobs into the pail.

Wendell said, "I heard the new Angus bull out at the Miller farm got too rambunctious. Heard he broke his dink."

They commented on that event and then walked over to our outhouse. They tried to tilt it off its hole, but disaster struck.

"Watch it, watch it, dammit it's falling!"

I said "dammit" to myself. I added that word to others that Norman and I practiced when we were outside.

The outhouse tilted and crashed to the ground. The roof separated so that nails were showing. I walked over to where Norman stood looking down into the old hole. We stared down at a moldy, unnatural mess that smelled.

"Get the hell back," Dad ordered.

Norman and I had already practiced the "hell" word.

Dad walked into the shack. A minute later he came out and emptied a bag of white lime into the hole. Wendell and Larry shoveled in dirt. Norman copied them using his shovel. I picked up clods with my left hand and threw them in.

The men rolled the outhouse over until it was next to the new hole. They cussed, yet managed to stand it upright. They tilted it back and forth until it sat over the new hole.

"Who's climbing up to pound in the nails?"

Larry balanced on an upside-down boiler and hammered in the outside nails. Then he went inside, and we heard pounding.

Norman picked up his shovel and helped Dad and Wendell scoop dirt around the outhouse. I watched a black locomotive race by with its pistons circling rapidly. I liked the way it announced itself with short blasts from its whistle. The locomotive pulled a string of boxcars, grain cars, flatbeds and oil tankers. Black smoke trailed the engine.

"Dammit, lost the hammer. Fell down the hole." Larry stuck his head out.

Again I mouthed the word "dammit" and enjoyed the feel of it.

Dad stepped into the outhouse. "If you can't reach it, we'll toss a kid down."

"Warren!"

Unaware that Dad called my name, I stood in a dusty hen's wallow, daydreaming. A scent of damp leaves reminded me of something, but I wasn't sure what. I wiped my runny nose on my sleeve, and then I felt Dad yank my arm. I let my body go limp as he pulled me into the outhouse. I felt my arms raised above my head. Then I slid down one of the two openings in the wooden bench.

The second before I dropped into the dirt hole, I glanced at my uncles. One leaned on his shovel and the other squatted on his heels. They smiled at me as they watched.

The dank smell and closeness of the black dirt scared me. I heard Dad yell, "Find the hammer. Hand it to me."

I bent my knees and brushed my hands around the loose dirt until they landed on the hammer. I stretched it to Dad's hand then stood still. I was scared that he would leave me. I wondered why Norman wasn't chosen.

Dad reached down, grabbed me and jerked me up. "Lunchtime," he said.

As Dad walked to the shack, he asked his brothers, 'You hear about that Wahoo farmer? Lost his chewing gum in the chicken pen. Thought he found it three times."

By bedtime, I could still picture that dirt hole, smell the oldness of it, and feel my fear. I could be happy just playing in the shack. As we walked in the back door, I noticed the orange-red sun. It appeared hazy, coated over by thin, autumn dust clouds. The tan cornfields nearby stood at attention.

Wann was a dying village but not yet a ghost town. Its size was three blocks long and three blocks wide. Cornfields framed three sides. The fourth boundary was the railroad tracks and sandpits on the west side. Seven miles south, the town of Ashland had become the main trading center for the Wann residents and the area farmers.

Looking around Wann a person would see shacks, junk piles, and see-through buildings. The men saw nothing but the end of another day during which they had survived with little regard for their future. They had dug the hole in time; in another month a freeze in the soil would bring a halt to shovel work.

I smelled meat frying in the kitchen. Mom stood at the cob-burning stove stirring bits of hamburger in white gravy. We washed at the sink pump. A kerosene lamp lighted the kitchen. The two younger brothers begged the uncles to toss them in the air. Mom was dark-haired, average height, but since Dad was a little over six feet, she only came up to his shoulder.

Each of us had a slice of home-made bread on a plate. Mom covered our bread with the hamburger gravy mixture. One slice only, no second helping, no dessert. There was water to drink. The table was small, so Mom stood by the stove and ate.

Before the uncles left, Larry said, "How about a game of shoe kick?"

After we trooped out the front door, the adults untied one of their shoes and lined up across the road. They held their shoe on their foot by cocking their toes up. One at a time, they swung their leg to see how far their shoe would fly. Norman and I practiced on the side.

Dad usually won, but this time the game turned against him.

"Come on, someone beat him!" Wendell and Larry shouted.

Mom made a lucky kick. Wendell and Larry cheered her. Dad tried too hard on his kick. His shoe slipped and angled off, way short of Mom's.

"Dammit all to hell."

After a laugh, Wendell and Larry shouldered their shovels and began the three-block walk to Grandpa's house at the other end of Wann.

Dad marched into our shack and told us to keep quiet.

By age six, I knew. I knew I was a sorry little mama's boy. I knew I was lazy, sickly, and finicky about food. I was vomity in the back seat of a car and walked with a limp from a deformed foot. I experienced headaches and felt pissed off too often.

The next day Dad drove away early. After a bowl of Oatmeal, Norman and I walked to the stockyards. We liked to climb the wooden railings and watch the freight trains rumble past.

Once a day, the Puddle Jumper train zipped through Wann. It had a diesel engine, Army green in color. It pulled a mail car and a passenger car. If it weren't unloading, it would race by so fast we couldn't study it.

This morning we saw blankets over in a corner under a short roof. We walked over and saw Uncle Wendell curled up. He opened his eyes, looked at us and smiled.

"Wha'cha doing?" Norman asked.

Wendell sat up and looked around. "Aw, your Grandpa kicked me out. Guess I'd been drinking too much beer, raising too much hell."

He was right about that. His ornery ways excited us. He said he didn't like school, didn't like to sit still.

"I skip school every chance I get."

After he had taken a leak, we made him walk to our shack. Mom gave him a piece of toast. Then we watched him grab his blankets and head toward Grandpa's house. He liked us, but we worried about what would become of him.

For supper that night we ate a slice of fried spam. The meat had a jelly feel to it. I was hungry so I managed to swallow all of it. Then there was a commotion at the door. We looked up at Dad, and he was whistling. He carried two brown sacks.

"Won a little at a poker game in Ashland. Got some groceries.

Hold it, hold it boys, don't rip those sacks."

I couldn't remember ever seeing so much foodstuff. Everything was store-bought, nothing homemade.

We helped unpack two loaves of white bread, two packages of minced ham, one ring of bologna, a small bag of cookies, two milk bottles, a box of Wheaties and cooking supplies like sugar and flour.

"Boys, you're drinking milk tonight."

Mom smiled at him. That puffed him up.

The last item he pulled out and held high—a Cracker Jacks box.

"All right boys, you get this if you ate your supper. But a little quiz first."

"Norman. Why do we save paper sacks?"

Norman grinned. "Do arithmetic on."

"Warren, what else do we use the sacks for?"

I wasn't paying attention. I turned over the Wheaties box to see if there was a mask on its back.

I felt Dad shake my shoulder. "Hey you, what do we use grocery sacks for, huh?"

I thought hard. Do adding on?"

"That's right, that's my boy."
"Okay boys, eat the Cracker Jacks, and I'll tell you about my next trip."

We grew up embracing the concept of finders' keepers. We were too young to consider the thin line between the luck of a discovery or theft. Once Dad had us sneak out after dark into a cornfield. He filled our arms with young field corn and then we snuck back.

"Boil it. Shake salt and pepper on it. Tastes as good as sweet corn."

One crisp fall night Mom told him the stove needed to be turned on.

"Send the boys out for cobs."

"No cob pile. You haven't brought any home yet."

"Oh hell. What about wood? We got any pieces of wood out back?"

Norman and I were sitting close, listening.

"No sticks of wood either."

"Dammit."

Dad glanced at us, and we could tell he was thinking of something to help us survive.

He pushed away from the table. "Get your jackets boys. We'll find something to burn."

We hurried to pull on our jackets and caps. Dad picked up a flashlight and a knife. Outside, he found two dusty gunnysacks.

"Carry your sacks and follow me. Keep quiet."

My heart pounded with excitement as we snuck through the tall weeds behind the shack.

Dad stopped and whispered to us, "There's a barbed-wire fence. I'll hold it up. You crawl under. Then we'll walk across the corn rows. Don't knock any over."

Cautiously, we followed Dad's light. The cornstalks were dry and slashed our faces.

Dad stopped. "Open your sacks. I'm going to throw corn in."

I glanced back. Two houses close to our shack had lights on. I didn't see anyone moving, but still my excitement mixed with dread.

Dad cut ears of corn until our sacks were half-full. We snuck back to the fence and into our home. We helped Dad remove the husks off several ears. He placed the dry husks in the bottom of our pot-bellied stove and lit them with a match. Then he placed four ears of corn on the fire.

"Boys, after the corn burns what's left?"

"The cob." Norman answered.

"And that'll burn too."

"Where'd you pick up a trick like that?" Mom asked him.

"Why, everyone knows during the depression farmers burned their corn for heat. Could only get two cents a bushel anyway."

We crowded close to the stove to listen to Dad.

"Tomorrow we're going to take couple buckets to the railroad tracks. Pick up any coal we find."

Mom said, "Why don't you go early so no one will see you? We don't want people to think we're poor."

"Okay, time for bed. Warren, get your butt in the kitchen."

Norman smiled his wide grin at me. He had light red hair like Dad's. My hair was a dark color like Mom's. In the kitchen there was a plate of cocoa butter melting on the stove.

"Sit up on the table. Take off your shoe and sock."

Dad tested the cocoa butter with his fingers. Then he sat down in front of me. He smeared the warm mixture over my left foot. He massaged the butter over the entire foot and in-between the toes.

"You remember how the doc said this will help your foot?"

I nodded my head, but how was I supposed to remember? I couldn't even remember having a cast put on or taken off.

"You know what happened when we brought you home?"

I shook my head.

"The cast was too tight. Your toes turned black and blue. I took scissors and cut the damn thing off. Took you back to the doctor the next day."

"Feel good?"

I nodded my head.

Dad grabbed a towel and wiped the cocoa butter off his hands and off my foot. We weren't raised to say thank you. Staying alive one more day, waiting for the gods of chance to smile on him with favor seemed to be his best bet and our best luck.

I went to our bedroom. There was one bed for Norman and me and one for the two youngest. When we moved into the shack, our folks had only one bed. Dad found used tires at the stockyards. He cleaned them up and put our mattresses on them. By this time, relatives had given us bedsteads.

    I thought Dad was exciting to be around. He knew how to survive. However, sometimes we experienced his temper. I liked Norman a lot too when we did things together. Sometimes he would piss me off though. When I ran to keep up with him, I would say I was the Lone Ranger. Then he would say he was since he was the fastest. Then I would stop trying since it didn't take long for my foot to ache.

CHAPTER FOUR

June 1989

I take a deep breath before I walk into my parent's apartment.

Mom arranged for a nursing home to accept Dad. His assets total a few dollars over zero. The home will take his social security check and give him thirty dollars a month. The state's Medicaid program will pay the rest of his monthly bill.

I worry about the final expenses knowing he has no life insurance. That seems strange since for a number of years, he was a successful insurance salesman. Mom appears uneasy. She points to his bedroom.

"Help him get dressed."

Another deep breath and then I walk into a room that has shoes and socks scattered, the bed unmade, and dresser drawers open. I recoil at the sight of an emaciated man. This is not my Dad, the large man who intimidated us boys when we were young.

He sits on the side of his bed with a sheet over his legs. He's wearing a white undershirt. Since that was one of his customs, you couldn't pay me to wear one. That was one part of my early rebellion.

He doesn't say much, so I don't either. He slides his watch on his bed stand. Then he moves his billfold to a new position. Next, he picks up a white hanky and then he shifts the watch back to its first location. I'm aware of a slight stench from his mattress.

I don't notice the shaking from Parkinson's which the doctor says is bringing him down. I don't know what to do since this is my first time of dealing with a weak person. Been lucky so far. Luck comes to mind since our family's life was influenced by luck, both good and bad.

Mom hands me a pair of white Jockey shorts.

"Help him," she says and turns away.

I kneel down and pull the shorts up over Dad's thin legs.

"Got to go," he says and motions to the bathroom.

I support one arm as he shuffles with baby steps toward the door. A minute later, "Help me up."

I go into his bathroom and think—this is what people do. I shouldn't think I would be immune all my life. People should help their elderly, I realize that. I grew up with a smart mouth, but I can't think of anything intelligent to say.

I'm thankful that Dad has pulled up his shorts. I try to lift him by one arm but can't. I have to reach around to his other side. It's like lifting a dead weight. He forgets to flush so I do it for him. I notice the hanging skin on his backside.

He quit the dentist so now he has few teeth. It must have become extremely difficult to eat, and he began to lose weight and strength. His lower face is pinched because of missing teeth. Next, I pull a white shirt over his sunken chest and help him button it.

Once again Dad rearranges his watch, billfold, and hanky. I wonder when was the last time he had his semi-circle of hair trimmed. It's uncombed and scraggly.

It's hard to believe that his life has come to this: This weak man who once was so powerful in my eyes. Who whipped me when I was young and sometimes deserving of a whipping. Who bullied me when I was a teenager.

Dad surprises me by voluntarily getting into my car. Mom sits in the back. I slide his walker into the trunk. I glance over at him as I drive. He knows he won't be living with Mom anymore. I worry if he will accept this move.

The home is red brick, four stories high, old but clean. I grab his walker and help him out of the car. Holding my breath, I walk beside him as he travels to the door. I'm thinking that once inside maybe the battle will be over. I wish I was going to the horse races with him instead of this.

Inside, an unpleasant odor lingers. An odor of oldness, of disease, of rotting death in a slop bucket. It's an odor of poverty. Dad glances around at the unfamiliar surroundings. I can't help but think that a nursing home is one of the saddest places in the world.

The staff treats him kindly as they place him in a room. It's a get-acquainted room, one of their nicer ones. No matter the niceties, the room with its dreary-colored brown shades and bedspread is discouraging. However, the room is warm, and I think this is where he might spend his last days.

Ken bursts into the room which causes Dad to smile. Ken hurries around the bed, over to the window, opens a closet. He can't stand still.

"Dad," he says, "I bet everything will work out fine. You'll only be here a short time. Once you get stronger, you'll move back."

I would like to think that way, but I'd bet against it.

Two minutes later, Kenny apologizes. "Dad, I have to see Barney out at the track. We got something going."

He rushes from the room. I'm surprised Dad didn't ask Ken to place a bet for him.

A nice-looking lady enters with a tray. Her experience shows as she soon has him sitting on the edge of the bed.

"Here's your lunch. A bowl of soup with coffee. Fruit for dessert."

I watch him pinch his thin lips, and I think, oh boy, here we go. His sales experience taught him to call people by their first name. He glances up at her name tag.

He asks, "Betty, what kind of apple pie do you have here?"

He tries to laugh, but the effort causes pain in his chest. His closed lips go in and out for a few seconds. He looks like he has been drinking sour milk. I have heard his joke many times before, I don't laugh. Mom turns her head toward the window.

Betty smiles, unfolds a napkin and hands it to him.

"Now Harry, don't be telling me all your jokes the first day."

He nods his head, pleased with himself, and then spoons most of the soup into his mouth.

A staff member helps him take off his shoes and sit up on the bed so they can take his blood pressure and temperature. When they leave he stays in that position. I stand by feeling helpless. I watch as he glances around the room. His mouth is half-open, easier to breath. Finally, he turns to me with that peculiar look of the elderly—confused, dazed, disoriented.

"I'm not staying here."

Mom lets out a cry, throws up her arms and rushes from the room. Now it's up to me. I glance out the window. I see people going about their business, not knowing or caring about this room's distress.

I think we are far away from the sweet madness and the glory of life outside. Love being kindled, beautiful babies being born, and some lucky humans dying without lingering. I would rather see Dad heading to the horse race track every day than down on his luck like this.

When I say nothing, Dad lays his head back and closes his eyes. His face is thin, and I'm sure he will look like this when we bury him. I have to fight the urge to let emotion overcome me. But the memories, oh, the memories are ever present.

I'm probably not the only person who has resented some of their father's actions. The feeling of hatred never entered my mind. Heck, he took us to Wells and Frost in Lincoln and bought us new shoes, didn't he. He taught us how to play poker and shoot pool. There were just too many times when I wished he had a steady job.

As I aged, a desire grew to separate myself from the horse races and from him. Long ago I set aside feelings of anger. Most of the time we considered ourselves a family since it was the only way of life we knew.

I decide to stay with him until I have no other choice. It was a hard thing to deliver him. It might be harder to walk out. He never hugged, never asked for forgiveness, I never heard him say to anyone, "I love you."

But Mom never said that either. Grandpa and Grandma Washburn never said it. Evidently the clan grew up repressing emotional expressions of love. What we did do was endure day by day.

Family actions and discussions were the order of the day. The depression of the '30s and the unwavering faith in gambling took a lot out of our family and Dad's family.

Finally, Dad looks over and says, "You know son, my life's been hard."

My mind brims over with recollections. But they seem irregular, curved, some run into others.

"Sure Dad, sure. But you were a survivor. I'll never forget how you doctored my club foot every night when I was little."

He lies back with a relaxed look. That must have been a significant memory for him.

"And remember Dad, living in that shanty in Wann. Remember how you stood up to old man Vosler when he accused you of stealing corn."

His eyes remain closed.

"And Dad, I'll never forget the time you got into a fight with that farmer in front of the general store."

That incident causes me to remember my brothers and I racing our bikes to the elevator where we hid to watch Dad beat up a farmer. I think he was arrested and taken to the Ashland jail. Now I wonder if that memory is correct. Did he actually spend a night in jail?

And in a whisper, "Thanks Dad, for rushing an attorney to our house that time a game warden tried to arrest me."

That event brings to mind one of his favorite sayings—"I've been accused a few times but never convicted."

He rests his head, eyes closed. I think he's asleep, so I pull a blanket over him. He doesn't move. I put my hand on his thin shoulder and keep it there. But what good does that do? Maybe just a final touch to say goodbye. Maybe we're reconciled, but the past can't be changed.

Darkness surrounds me as I stumble outside. I drop my head and try to hide my face. Dammit, I can't help it. He is my Dad, faults and all, but who doesn't have them. Let them cast the first stones.

I shouldn't think it strange that tears flow as conflicting emotions overwhelm me. Mom and I are silent as I drive her to their apartment. Then I drive home wishing Dad could have gone to a horse race track forever and ever. I know that made him happy.

1946-47

By 1947, we had lived in the shanty for three years. The historical events of the late '40s didn't touch our lives. So the end of World War II, the Marshall Plan, the red scare of communism, they didn't affect us. Day by day survival gave us worries enough. Polio was one of the worst fears of parents.

One October day Norman and I played outside making a fort out of a cardboard box. The neighbor across the road, old man Vosler, moseyed into our yard.

"Where's your dad?"

Norman ran inside while I stared at Vosler. He wore bib overalls but the feature I glanced at was a purple wart next to his nose. He smelled of fried onions.

Dad walked out wearing his white shirt and blue slacks.

Vosler said, "Your five dollar rent was due last week."

I pulled our red wagon away, but I was all ears, hoping to learn new cuss words.

"You always got paid before didn't you? You'll get your money. Just settle down before you really piss me off."

I could tell Vosler didn't want an argument. However, he was a sly old horse trader Grandma had told us.

He said, "Okay, that's fine, just fine."

Vosler studied the shanty for a few seconds then added, "Can remember when I used to raise chickens in there."

Vosler was bigger and older than Dad. Suddenly, Dad's fist was in Vosler's face.

"Listen here, you mention those damn chickens once more and I'll slap you silly, understand?"

Old man Vosler turned and began to shuffle across the road to his house. Grandma said Vosler had a hitch in his giddyup, whatever that meant.

Then he turned back and said, "Was up to the general store this morning. Seems as if a story going round that Allington had the county sheriff out yesterday. Something about missing corn."

Then Vosler glanced at the cornfield that marked the southern end of Wann. The field ran along his backyard and our back weed patch. I kept myself from looking at Dad, didn't want to give anything away.

Dad hesitated for a few seconds, then, "Hah, you better get up earlier in the morning if you're gonna try to bullshit me."

Dad stepped toward Vosler.

"Now, got news for you. What's the name that brown dog of yours, Rex isn't it? Did you hear him yelp when I put a load of buckshot up his hinny? My chicken count went down by two last week. You got any story on that?"

Vosler folded his arms inside his overalls and gave up. Dad glared at him until he walked away. Dad went back into our shack. Yeah, Dad showed him. Wouldn't bet against Dad if I had a hundred dollars.

I knew he didn't back down from anyone. I didn't learn any new cuss words, already knew pissed off, damn, and bullshit.

I liked to listen to older people talk. I hated being left out on anything. There were always signs. Relatives would talk softly or look at us kids before they discussed something important.

Once I heard Mom say, "Harry, the boys are getting a slice of toast with strawberry jam for lunch. All we got. Nothing for supper."

Dad sat and stared at the sink pump. Then he held his head in his hands.

"Maybe you can borrow a little from your folks for groceries."

"No, dammit, already owe them too much."

"Can't you ask for some eggs? I can scramble them for supper."

"Dammit to hell. I'm going to Memphis. Might have luck playing poker."

Dad returned after dark, barging in the back door. He carried a rifle which he stood next to the sink. He grabbed a kitchen knife then disappeared. We sat and looked at each other and no longer felt hungry.

A few minutes later he walked in carrying two skinned rabbits.

"Have any luck?" Mom asked.

"Hah. Yeah, I had luck, bad luck. Lost my last two dollars. Came back and borrowed dad's rifle. Got these two over by the sandpits. Boys can eat fried rabbit tonight."

The fried rabbit aroma roused my taste buds. The rabbit meat tasted good, but I didn't eat much. I was finicky, and if something didn't suit me, I'd let my stomach shrink another fraction of an inch.

While we were eating Dad announced, "If I could get a stash together, I'd buy that bookie joint in Ashland. Could run it better than those numbskulls."

"Thought that was illegal."

"Aw hell, no one pays any attention. They haven't shut down the blockhead running it now. No way would they catch me."

"Hells bells, boys," he said, "if I ran that business we wouldn't be on the short end of the stick. We'd ride the gravy train with cherry pie for wheels."

The next day he left early but drove up in his Chevy after we finished lunch. We ate homemade bread from Grandma with the rest of the rabbit pieces.

"Okay boys. Sit on the couch. Divide this box of Cracker Jacks. Don't move 'til I tell you to. If someone comes to the door give me a holler."

Dad disappeared into the bedroom. Cracker Jacks was a whopping treat for us. Norman gave each the same amount. After we had stuffed our mouths, I looked at him. His puzzled look scared me.

I remembered that anytime adults acted strange or exchanged knowing looks, then uncertainty entered our lives. We sat quietly and looked out the window as a rain shower began. The wind rattled the door and windows, yet I could hear hushed noises coming from the bedroom.

To hell with it, I thought, I'm a little sneak anyway, once more won't hurt. I stood up, looked at my brothers and placed a finger on my lips. I tiptoed from the room into the kitchen. I hesitated for a second when a floorboard creaked.

I tip-toed into our bedroom. Then I edged close to the slat partition. I peeked through a slender gap. I saw a bare arm and movement under an upraised blanket. I was scared but excited and dumb as to what was happening. I had watched adults when they hugged, kissed, and laughed, but this action was new.

I watched for a minute, then I tip-toed back through the kitchen. When I reached the couch, Norman whispered, "What's happening?"

"I think they're hugging in bed."

1947-48

By the time I was seven, I realized that Dad didn't allow any independent thoughts or spoken opinions that didn't agree with him. If he thought something was funny, all of us laughed. I could tell Mom supported him outwardly, but there were times when I didn't like the way he treated her.

Wann's elementary school sat in the middle of Wann. The windows were high enough so that we couldn't look out and become distracted by scenes of the world. Norman and I walked the block and a half in the morning, then home for lunch and back to school, and then home after school.

In the cold winter of 1947, our lunch was one boiled wiener on a half slice of bread. For the afternoon recess, all the boys bundled up and went outside to run up and down the snowdrifts.

After a few minutes of play Norman ran by me and yelled, "There's Dad."

I saw Dad's black Chevy moving past the school, so I ran after Norman. Norman yelled and waved, but Dad didn't honk at him. I ran behind Norman until I fell down in the snow. When I looked up, Dad had turned the corner toward the general store. I wiped the snow and snot on my sleeve. Then back to the classroom to read— "See Dick, see Jane. See Dick and Jane."

It was a wintry December day, gray and still during the daylight hours. The dark storm clouds mingled low over Wann. Bare trees stood frozen at attention. I didn't see any of Roy Everman's Rhode Island Red chickens running around as usual. *Must be staying in their coops*, I thought.

After school Norman and I shuffled home through the snow and the darkening twilight. Our heads bent into the cold to keep our bare necks warm. Our brown caps had the earmuffs pulled down, but they didn't cover all of our face or neck. I liked the way the cold air froze the inside of my nose.

It was just the two of us, the only living, moving beings as we passed four houses that seemed to shiver. At least our stove gave some warmth; it was all I looked forward to after enduring the pain of the zero degree cold--just to make it into our house.

"Leave your jackets on," Mom said as she met us at the door.

"Why?" I asked. I wanted to tell her something about school.

"I want you boys to go up to Grandpa's and get a load of cobs."

"It's too cold. Where's Dad?"

"He went to the horse races in Hot Springs, Arkansas."

So that's it, he's gone again, leaving us with no cobs. I regretted ever opening my mouth when I saw the wet-eyed look on Mom's face. It scared me. It was just another fear to fill a shelf in my cupboard of nightmares.

The awful truth was this: Dad left the family without a bite to eat. The table, the icebox, the food shelves were empty and a bitter night was settling down. I could barely feel any heat from our black stove. A light was shining from a table lamp, but that was all to sustain our existence.

Mom bent down towards us. I saw a couple of tears. It was a scary moment when she cried right in front of us.

"Get some food also." She managed to whisper while holding on to our shoulders.

Dad didn't stack a pile of cobs for the winter; maybe he was too busy. Once a week, Norman and I would place a cardboard box on our sled. We would pull the sled three blocks to Grandpa's cob shed.

The road was never cleared off, just ice and snow-packed, making sledding easy. Few cars ever appeared on our roads, so we didn't have to worry about traffic.

Mon composed herself and said, "Go get a load of cobs. Ask for five eggs. Otherwise we won't have supper. There's nothing to eat here."

I thought, *for crying out loud! Five eggs? For five of us?* I guessed we would each have a few bites.

"Will you boys do that?" She asked.

Norman shook his head. I knew what was coming. Dad runs away, Mom and Norman have too much pride to beg relatives. Her eyes turned toward me, to the skinny, sick, lazy kid, who harbored no pride whatsoever.

"Ask for five eggs," She pleaded to me.

How could I let her down? What was I suppose to do? Suddenly develop principles from Dad's example? I nodded my head. I knew her hopes. Maybe in a few days she would receive a letter with a few dollar bills, maybe even a five. Then we would have food for another week.

Once again into the frosty air we plodded, taking turns pulling the sled. Cold pains are not much different from hunger or heartache pains. All of them teach endurance.

We headed down the street straight for Grandpa's house. Past the now quiet, grey stone three-room schoolhouse. Past a small, red brick building that used to be the Bank of Wann back in the "pioneer glory days." A building to which we would move to the next year.

We turned into Grandpa's lane, skirted the red barn and pulled our sled into the cob shed. It was getting late; half of the inside was in shadows. I liked the cob smell, musty but a smell I wanted to taste. We were out of the winter's cold at least. I wondered if we would discover a mason jar full of silver coins. We had seen Grandpa pull a jar out of the cob pile last year.

We scooped up the cobs and filled the box. Norman maneuvered the sled while I steeled myself for what I had to do. I HAD TO DO IT! We moved out to the driveway, Norman pulled and I pushed. He stopped, and we looked toward Grandma's house where a faint light materialized through the kitchen window.

"Go do it," Norman said. He hung on to the sled rope as if he had to stay with the main job.

I was colder than cold and hungry as hell. I felt ticked off that of all the beggars in the world, it was me who had to announce to the grandparents that their oldest son couldn't feed his family.

The resolution in my backbone struggled with the dread in my heart as I climbed up the steps and opened the kitchen door. Grandma looked at me from in front of her kitchen stove. I pulled off my cold mittens and felt the terrible guilt of being ashamed.

I asked, "Can Mom borrow five eggs?"

"Do you have any bread?" Grandma asked.

"Don't know."

Grandma was frying pork chops and the heavenly aroma filled my nose. My mouth watered while hunger pangs came to the forefront. Grandpa walked into the kitchen in time to hear my timid plea. He looked out the door and called Norman to come in and warm up.

Norman was Grandpa's oldest grandson and he showed signs of becoming a worker. My mind was not on work, more like getting out of it. I was too much of a sick slacker for Grandpa.

Norman spoke up, "Guess we kinda been hungry for a day. Dad's gone."

I moved out of the way for Norman. Grandma and Grandpa were talking, but I didn't listen. I stared at the brown grocery sack they filled with food staples--more than I could remember seeing for a long time.

Grandpa loaded the bag on the back of the sled and sent us on our way. What would Mom think? We hustled all the way home. We were anxious to get out of the cold and hungry for any food.

Still, I felt depressed wondering how we could repay our grandparents. I hated having to do what I had done. I never wanted to beg again.

I thought our grandparents were angels. Mom cooked well when she had food supplies. That night, thanks to our grandparents, we huddled against the cold and the gloom of the land but not against hunger pangs. No, for a couple of days having a bite to eat diminished our hunger.

Before I went to bed, I remembered what I wanted to tell Mom.

"Mom, I had a problem in school. The teacher gave us scissors, but mine wouldn't cut paper."

"Did you tell her?"

"She took the scissors out of my left hand and put them in my right hand. She said I had to learn to cut that way."

"When you were little you would pick up a play hammer in your left hand, but your Dad would take it away and put it in your right. Then you would throw it away and cry. Finally, we realized you were left-handed. But at school you'll have to learn to use the right-handed scissors."

"That's not fair."

"But you're smart enough. Just practice for a while and you'll do it."

That night I thought about Dad. Where did he get money for gas to drive to Arkansas, how would he buy meals?

CHAPTER FIVE

JULY 1989

I wondered if Dad could adjust to living in a home and Mom adjust to living alone.

I decided to see Dad the following weekend. If everything were going well, twice a month would be enough. My thoughts drifted toward Mom. She graduated from Ashland high school in the late '30s. She earned money by cleaning houses and being a waitress while living with her family.

When she would talk about her wedding day, I could never judge her feelings. Was she feeling sorry for herself or trying to make the best of a difficult situation?

Dad was down on luck at that time. The few dollars he earned from selling eggs or setting up a fruit stand were soon lost at the races.

"How'd you get married, Mom?"

She said Grandpa Sam drove Dad and her to Lincoln in August of 1938. Her sister and husband were witnesses. A justice of the peace married them while Grandpa took a nap in his panel truck.

"Where did you live?"

"We drove to the Washburn farm near Ashland. That afternoon the family picked tomatoes, so I helped. We lived in their family house. The next day Sam and Harry drove to Lincoln to sell the tomatoes. That was our life."

Driving to see Dad, I wondered if I'd have enough guts to ask him the big question—how he became a gambler. I used to speculate about it. Then I went off to college, married, got a job and moved away.

I wondered if he'd answer me honestly or would he make something up. Probably piss him off because he'd think I was questioning him. That was something unheard of when I was young. I never confronted him. My only plan was to remove myself physically.

In the home, he was sitting up in bed. Maybe he appeared weaker than before; maybe he had lost weight.

"You remember living in that old shack?" He asked.

"Sure Dad. I remember the time you dropped me down the outhouse hole. And the kick-the-shoe game you played with your brothers and Mom. Norman and I started school from that shack."

"What about that time, Dad, when we borrowed field corn to burn in our stove?"

He smiled. Possibly that old memory made him happy.

We visited for an hour then Mom motioned me out into the hall.

"He's failing a bit."

"Maybe, but he doesn't look too bad. Doctor say anything?"

She hesitated before answering, "He won't make it back to the apartment."

Driving home, more memories surfaced.

1948

Some might think that our lives were depressed, living in that shanty during the long winters. Grey clouds covered the sky. Wild birds would haunt Wann for a while before moving on.

At times we waded through knee-deep snow drifts. And yet, if we could gather around Mom for warmth and have a few clothes to wear and food to eat, we expected nothing more. The days of growing up in Wann rolled into weeks and the weeks into months.

Except for Dad, none of us left Wann. The cold and snow would trap us indoors for days. The worst storms would blow snowflakes through the rafters, and we would wake up and brush them off our blankets.

Wann was small enough that every dog ran freely. There weren't many cats in the village. Maybe Rex killed them as Dad thought he killed chickens. The few people who raised chickens for eggs or for frying let them free range also. The playground where we played football and baseball would have a few of Everman's red chickens scratching in the weeds until we ran out for recess.

One summer morning Dad said, "Norman and Warren, walk with me to the store."

From the shanty, he headed for the back path that went by the stockyards and the elevator. Cars rarely used this way; weeds had overgrown the trail. We had walked a block when Dad leaned down into a ditch and pulled out a dead chicken.

"Dammit, I'll bet that damn dog of Vosler's killed this one."

The chicken did look like one of ours. Dad carried it to the store and threw it down by the gas pump. Grandpa and Grandma were running the store at this time. Dad marched in, saw old man Vosler and began to give him hell. A couple of farmers were there, so they joined the debate, as did Grandpa Sam.

The store had wooden floors and a pot-bellied stove situated in the middle. Grandpa stood behind the counter. Toward the back was a meat cooler and a soda pop container. A door led to the other half of the white board building. That's where Grandpa and Grandma lived. It had indoor plumbing and an upstairs.

Norman and I stopped by the candy counter to stare and dream. We discussed which candy bar we would buy if we had a nickel. The majority of the time neither of us had a red cent.

The Snickers bar looked the biggest, but I craved the pieces of the Bit-O-Honey. There were penny candy pieces, so we debated if five of something would be better than one bar. Then I saw a packet of Walnettos and decided that's what I would buy.

Besides shooting Rex, the men voiced their opinions on how to stop him. I kinda liked the dog; he was easy to pet and seemed to have a smile on his face.

Finally, one of the farmers, Rieken or Allington said, "Bet a dollar I can cure that dog."

Dad took the bet, never knew him to back down.

All of us trooped outside. Dad picked up the chicken and handed it to the farmer. Norman captured Rex in a nearby field. The farmer fetched a short length of rope from his pickup. He laid the dead chicken on Rex's back and secured it with the rope. Then he said, "Okay, let the dog go."

Rex jumped around in circles and almost broke his neck trying to bite the chicken. Finally, he sped down the block and out of sight as if speed could outrun the torment attached to him.

During the next days, we would spot Rex off in the distance, acting agitated. When we came close we could smell the ripe chicken and see its grayish green color. At the end of a week, Vosler pulled the chicken off, and we watched Rex for a while. If a chicken came close, he took off lickity-split in the other direction. The farmer won his bet.

Dad said, "He'll have to look me up if he wants paid."

Norman soon began to enjoy the responsibilities of a first-born. He thrived on the attention from Mom and Dad and from the grandparents. He always appeared happy and curious. However, sometimes Norman overdid things.

In the middle of our shanty's front room sat a potbelly stove. When the stove was in use, Dad would empty the ashtray that sat underneath. He carried it to an ash pile near the outhouse. Once a week he shoveled the cold ashes against the foundation of the shanty. Helps keep out the cold wind he said.

Dad drove to the Omaha bookies this day. Mom walked a block to visit with Mrs. Lehr. Norman looked around to do something that would bring him praise. I saw an old funny book beneath the bed, so I crawled under to get it.

Norman studied the stove for a bit before making up his mind. He struggled with the ashtray but managed to get it outside without scattering ashes on the floor. Forgetting about the pile, he emptied the ashes across the shack's foundation, on top of other ashes. Then he replaced the tray under the stove.

Later Mom said she was visiting but began to wonder why Mrs. Lehr wasn't talking or looking at her. The neighbor lady frowned over Mom's shoulder and suddenly screamed, "Look!"

Mom turned and saw a column of smoke billowing up from the back of our shanty. I heard her tell relatives she thought she peed her pants as she dropped flowers and raced home yelling "Fire! Fire!"

The ashes that Norman emptied had live embers in them. Next to the clapboard, it didn't take long for them to ignite. Mr. Everman and Vosler came running with pails of water. Mom ran in the front door, grabbed her two youngest and pulled them out to the road. Then she ran around to the back to see Norman yanking the pump handle up and down to fill a water pail.

My head was in the comic book, Uncle Scrooge and Donald Duck. I didn't pay any attention to the smoky smell or the noise. When Vosler came into the kitchen for another bucket of water, he saw me leaning against a counter. Rudely, he grabbed my arm and yanked me out the back door.

"Get the hell out of there boy. What's wrong with you?"

Someone made an emergency call on the party telephone line, then more people showed up to help. The smoldering ashes had water splashed on them. Men with shovels and rakes pulled ashes away from the foundation. The clapboards were drenched with water. Soon the smoke faded away.

Norman wasn't whipped. When Mom explained the mistake he made, Norman's face turned into a sickly grin. As for me, I hadn't liked old man Vosler for awhile. Now I retained an extreme dislike of him.

In the last year of the shanty, all of us caught chicken pox. Norman and I missed a week of school. A farm girl caught polio and came home in braces.

Mom told us that we were due to move to a bigger house. She wondered why we still lived in a shack while the economy boomed and new houses appeared in Ashland. Farmers drove newer pickups and the rich talked about a new invention called a television.

Before they were married, Mom knew Dad managed his life mostly by gambling. He would take her on a date to the horse races in Omaha and Lincoln. He was an excellent student of the Daily Racing Form, the Blue Sheet, and the race program.

Dad was wise in the ways of picking winning horses. His study of the horse's past performance was smart. How long was the race, what was the weather condition, who was the jockey, and what was the opposition. His main problem was gathering enough cash from his previous winnings and from relatives.

Sometimes he hit it big. If Mom were along, he promised to take her the next time. If he lost, it was because he lost his lucky pen or didn't have on his lucky hat. Maybe Mom was to blame. Twice he postponed their wedding because he was broke. Then he hit a lick, and the wedding was on.

During one week snowstorms closed down the village. In the shack with four boys day after day, Mom became depressed and fell ill.

One afternoon she said to Dad, "Must have the flu. Going to bed. Can you watch the boys for an hour or so?"

Dad bundled us with jackets, gloves, and caps. He tied a diaper over his head and ears and under his chin. Then he placed his grey hat on his head.

He found an old sled and gave us rides in the road, two at a time. After he pulled us as fast as he could, he would make a sharp turn, spilling us into the snow. We jumped up laughing with snow in our faces, but begged for another ride. Our cheeks were pink when we went indoors.

Dad said, "Get your jackets off and sit at the table. 'Bout time you learned to play cards."

He found a deck and pulled out a box of matches from a cupboard.

"Okay boys, you each get fifteen to bet with. Let's see who can win."

We piled our matches and then watched him shuffle the cards.

"Now," he said, "this game is called high-card poker. We each get three cards. Then we bet. Whoever has the highest card wins the pot. Norman, what's the highest card in the deck?"

"The king."

"Nope. Warren, what's the highest card?"

Hell, I didn't know, and I didn't care. Why didn't we just start playing I wondered?

"I don't know," I said, "whatever you want it to be."

"Don't be a little smart ass or you'll get the yardstick. The ace is the highest card. Now, everyone put one match in the center pot. That's called the ante."

We put one match in, but I was pouting since he called me a smart ass. I slouched down in my chair and didn't look at him.

"Everyone gets three cards, and now we bet. Don't show your cards to anyone. Remember, high card wins the pot."

"I bet one," I said since I had a queen. My three brothers didn't bet, but Dad said, "I'll call you which means I'll put one in also. Okay, what ya got?"

I smiled as I turned my cards over and said, "Got a queen."

Dad said, "My king beats your queen. So I get the pot."

"Dammit," I blurted out and got a slap across my shoulder.

"Watch your mouth."

I learned that word from him but thought I'd better not mention that fact.

Norman won the next hand with a ten. A few hands later I was down to seven matches, but one of my cards was the king of spades.

"I'll bet three."

Dad called me again and asked what my highest was.

"A king, the winner."

"Hold on," he said, "I have an ace."

I threw the rest of my matches to the center of the table and stormed outside. I felt like crying.

When I came back, Dad had put the cards and matches away. He told us to watch this new trick. He sat a water glass in the middle of the table, and then he placed a spoon face up in front of the glass. Next, he inserted the handle of a fork under the mouth of the spoon.

When he struck his fist down on the fork, the spoon flew up and turned over. On his third try, the spoon landed in the glass. We laughed and then Norman wanted to try.

Dad set the spoon and fork in place and then Norman pounded his fist down on the fork. The spoon flew straight into the glass and shattered it, broken shards flying everywhere. One piece of glass hit me right between my eyes.

I felt a slight sting, so I reached up and pulled the glass chip off. Blood began to run down my face. Dad yelled for Mom. Norman tried to pick up broken glass. Mickey and Kenny scampered into the next room.

I stood there, dumb, wondering about the blood but not feeling a lot of pain. One thing I knew for sure, the wound would have to heal on its own, no doctor visits for the Washburn boys. A week later a small scar remained between my eyes.

Across the path from our shanty sat a large house which had indoor plumbing and an upstairs. While our shanty had parts of chicken wire running around the yard, this house had an iron fence. A young woman and her two sons moved into that house.

The woman was short and friendly to everyone. Her two sons were the same age as my younger brothers, so we played together in their yard. We would toss a football up, and then try to tackle the man with the ball.

They had a porch light, so we would play there after dark, no matter how cold. One day we noticed a man living there, a big man, taller than Dad. Clouds of uncertainty moved over Wann then.

Shortly thereafter a surprising quietness invaded Wann. My

brothers and I were at odds with each other. The biggest hint of something going to happen was the way the adults exchanged quiet words after glances toward us.

Something unusual was going to take place. The feeling came over me after a potato soup lunch, but I forget about it until Dad gathered the family about four o'clock and told us, "We're going to walk up to Grandpa's for supper."

Grandma fixed egg sandwiches. The adults told us to go outside and play. The sun sat early and twilight rushed in soon after. Suddenly two carloads of relatives pulled into Grandpa's driveway. Most of the time when this happened, it was a joyous occasion. This time everyone was hushed up about something.

I looked over at the Wann Christian Church and noticed a line of cars. Once parked, their lights shut off immediately. Some of us jogged up Grandpa's lane toward the church. At the end of the lane we stopped and I looked passed the church toward the general store. More cars were parking, people were getting out, some were carrying things.

A cloudy darkness settled over Wann as we raced back to the house. Only to be met by the entire Washburn clan. Mom and Dad told us to follow along, but stay behind them and keep quiet.

When we reached the road, we joined with the farmers who had already parked their cars. The group walked south down the main Wann road. Those who had parked by the store were walking in the same direction, only on the path that went passed the elevator.

Our clan snuck along with the farmers' families, the elderly, and the kids. It became a migration of silent souls. The secrecy caused my heart to race. I was surprised my stomach didn't churn up and vomit right there.

Finally, this mass of humanity reached the rich house that was showing lights through its windows. The advance troops stopped in the dark shadows near the iron fence. I made sure I stayed close to Mom.

I watched the bravest sneak through the fence using the yard trees to hide them. A few of them crept up to the house and ducked down under the windows. The air around us became still, intense with suspense. It felt like the Hungarian bull from the Veskerna farm was squatting on my chest.

I didn't know if God in his glory was structuring a brief moment of paradise or if the devil was going to make an appearance to strike us down for our wrongdoing. I figured we must be doing something wrong or else why all the secrecy.

Then it happened. An explosion of sounds with the WHAM, WHAM, WHAM of shotgun blasts.

Shotguns flamed, pots and pans rang out, bells clanged, and people yelled. Dad had brought a large cowbell from Grandpa's, and he was shaking it. I joined with the screaming just to stop the tension if nothing else. What a racket! On and on it continued.

"Mom, what's happening?"

"Everyone is welcoming the new couple; it's a Shivaree in their honor."

Soon the excitement subsided. The couple opened their doors. People trooped in and out, everyone happy about the entire episode. Tubs of beer bottles appeared in the back yard. Kids ran in the house and out the back door. However, on my second pass through the kitchen, I saw something that stopped me dead in my tracks.

Stacks of candy bars covered one counter. I didn't see any sign that read five cents each. I ran to Mom to ask her if everyone, even kids, would get a free one. She said she thought so. I was close to the front of the line since I had never heard of a free candy bar before.

I have to admit that my mind considered the possibility of some people getting two bars if there were extras. Anyway, it was a happy night for all. The Shivaree was a perfect example of Wann entertainment, home-made from the get-go. However, after we went to bed, I wondered about one thing.

"Dad, how's come that family had all those candy bars in their kitchen?"

All he said was, "You're smart enough. Figure it out for yourself."

CHAPTER SIX

1948-49

In late fall of 1948, Norman and I jogged home from school one day to find the shack in an uproar.

"We're moving!" Mom cried out.

She had packed our clothes in peach baskets and cardboard boxes.

"Where to? When we moving?"

"Tomorrow. To the bank building."

In the distant past, settlers had built a red-brick building and named it The Bank of Wann. One of Dad's sisters had lived in the bank. Her husband moved them to Denver for his new job. Grandpa owned the property and charged ten dollars a month for rent.

One block north of the bank was the Wann Christian Church. The general store was one block west. Across the road to the east were Grandpa's sweet corn and strawberry fields. His house and outbuildings sat at the north border of his fields.

"You boys wear the same clothes tomorrow. I'll pack you a lunch to eat. After school walk to the bank building. Don't come back to this rat hole."

I thought that life was looking up for us. I knew the bank had electricity, a newer outhouse, and a bright red outdoor pump. Then Dad walked in the door.

"Car broke down. Can't fix it."

I was getting pissed off at all the negative news he delivered. Moreover, I inherited his quick temper; therefore, I had problems with my smart mouth. But I was no match for him. It took me a long time to learn that.

"How we going to move? We're supposed to tomorrow."

"You're supposed to keep your mouth shut unless you want a whipping."

Well, he had a valid point. But I was getting older, and liked to taunt him a little. I was careful not to push him too far. His good humor could only last so long.

He said, "We can't borrow Sam's truck. He's going to Omaha. I'll rig something up."

I brooded during supper which was fried eggs. I could eat them scrambled but not fried or poached. When Dad wasn't watching, I ducked my head and held my nose, then swallowed pieces of egg. If I couldn't smell it, I couldn't taste it.

The next morning we ate a bowl of Cream O' Wheat, and then Norman and I walked to school. We were anxious to tell the other kids. When some asked where we were moving, I said to Lincoln or Omaha. I liked the notoriety.

During the morning recess, we noticed kids pointing at something in the road. We ran over to look, and my heart dropped. They were commenting about Mom and Dad.

Dad pulled our red wagon loaded with cardboard boxes. Mom carried a wooden peach basket full of clothes. Mickey and Kenny walked behind her. *So that's the way Dad figured out how to move*, I thought.

We heard Wayne Nast, "Hey look! We got gypsies in Wann."

When he saw Norman walking towards him, Wayne began to edge away.

Norman yelled, "Come here you little chickenshit if you ain't scared."

I watched Norman run down Wayne. Kids gathered around, anxious to see a fight. Then the teacher I loved, Miss Barta, stepped outside and rang the bell.

Norman turned eight that year. He was tough, loved to get into fights. I turned seven, and the little brothers were four and five. I tried to avoid fights. There were a couple of farm girls who could wrestle me down if they wanted. They always ran at me when we played Red Rover.

After school we ran to the bank building. Grandpa had returned, so Wendell and Larry helped move our beds, table, and chairs. The inside of the bank was smaller than the shack. There was only room for two beds, so Norman and I slept on a pullout couch.

That night I thought about our shack. Figured I would never step inside it again, and I was right. I remembered our family living there and repressed the hard times.

In our new house, I felt a chapter in our life had ended. I was happy, but a sense of sadness mixed with it. It was like messing with a loose tooth. Wiggling it back and forth brought a little pain but also felt good.

Anyway, I was too tender-hearted. I felt sorry for the toads and snakes we clubbed to death. I thought the animals were doing what animals should be doing. Then for no reason at all, we murdered them.

When I thought things over, I realized I didn't know much. I thought Grandma liked me, I knew Mom did, and Miss Barta, my teacher, was special. I wasn't strong physically and wasn't real strong mentally unless I lost my temper. Anyway, I felt sad about leaving the shack. It was where my memory of our family began.

I was proud that our family survived the hunger, lack of money, and the cold of winter. However, this new building had bright light bulbs. Mom appeared happy. Since Dad was sleeping here, I felt secure with the newness of it all.

Our lives changed overnight. Dad sat a radio on top of the icebox. When we listened to *Gangbusters*, I stood on a chair to watch the radio and listen, all tensed up.

Fibber McGee and Molly sounded funny. A few years later *Gunsmoke* came on with Marshal Dillon and Miss Kitty. We never missed *The Lone Ranger and Tonto*.

Dad bought a used record player and borrowed records from his folks. He played "Blue Moon of Kentucky" and "Goodnight Irene". He whistled along with the tunes. He hung his two favorite paintings on a wall. One was a mountain scene with a covered wagon train kicking up dust. The other was a black wolf standing on a snow-covered ridge looking down on a ranch house.

Soon after our move, Dad hit a lick and Mom got her first used Singer Sewing machine. I figured that we would be up to our ears in candy and soda pop. But he had a surprise. He brought home a bottle of cod liver oil. "Good for your health and bowels," he told us. I puked up the first tablespoon he emptied into my mouth. Plus what I had eaten that morning.

"Next time you do that, you get the belt."

By Thanksgiving the weather kept us indoors and shut down the school. The heavy wet snow piled up. The drifts along the tree lines were higher than our heads.

We sat at the front window to watch the snow swirl. I thought the wind was attacking our building. Then we would sit with blankets over our heads. Sometimes, instead of falling down, the snow would blow horizontally across the window.

Grandpa walked over one afternoon to tell us the temperature was twenty below last night. Once we woke to find snow had blown under our door. We saw our breath since the oil stove had quit working. Dad took an old towel, rolled it up, and stuffed it under the door.

"Norman, it's your job to do this every night. You better not forget and I don't mean maybe."

When Dad fired up the stove, we climbed out of bed. We wrapped blankets around us and stood next to the stove until it got too hot. When it warmed up, we dressed and walked down the road past the school building. Houses had drifts up to their windows and roofs had snow piled high. Neighbors were out with shovels making the path to the outhouse a bit easier.

Grandpa owned two turkeys which strutted around his yard as if they owned it. It scared me when they raised their heads and looked me straight in the eye. Grandpa named one Truman and the other Dewey. Whichever man lost the election meant that turkey would be the Thanksgiving meal.

We played indoor games or else Mom read to us. We played hide the thimble and Tiddly-Winks. If we had enough sheets of paper, we would play battleship. We drew two grids of ten vertical lines and crossed them with ten horizontal lines. We hid our ships on one grid and fired at the ships on the other grid. Nobody liked dominoes as much as I did. So we didn't play it too often.

On winter nights if the God of fortune smiled on us, a special treat materialized. Mom heated the kitchen stove. In her skillet she blended sugar, a cocoa mixture, and milk until it bubbled. If we had collected enough black walnuts, we cracked them open on the kitchen counter. Mixed with the fudge, the nut meat added a crunchy flavor.

While this was going on, her four boys surrounded her.
"My turn to stir."
"My turn to toss in the walnuts."
"Ain't neither."
"Is so."
We argued as to who was the first to lick the spoon and clean out

the skillet after Mom poured the fudge into a cake pan.

After an hour in the icebox, the fudge hardened, and Mom cut squares for us. A king never lived better. We didn't think about future cavities. When we went to bed the flavor of sugary, chocolate, black walnut homemade fudge lingered long into our happy dreams.

Behind the general store there stood a wilderness of cottonwoods, elms and oak trees. Branches had fallen, rotten limbs hung down, and the ground was covered with leaves, dead branches, and pieces of forgotten farm machinery from three generations ago. You could just barely see skeletons of abandoned cars.

A small house stood in the center of this thicket. It used to be the Wann Post Office and it was as old as the surrounding trees. It didn't have a door, glass was broken out of windows, and there was fallen plaster over the floors. There was animal droppings in every room.

We awoke one morning to the sound of axes striking trees in that vicinity. A family of Arkansas squatters had moved in overnight. It was the Shultz family, headed up by Axel Shultz. The kids who came to school were Other, Athern, Martion, Betty, and Pauline.

Other was in my grade. Other's arms were like iron rods, probably from chopping wood since he was two. Other took a dislike to me, probably because I made fun of his ignorance. Therefore, whenever he got the chance, he would plow his iron fist into my skinny arm.

In the middle of a late November night, a light turned on. I struggled to open my eyes from what felt like gravel sticking them closed. Mom was pulling on her coat. Hurry up she told Dad while he was on the phone. Norman asked what's happening. Mom opened the door and walked out. Dad hung up the phone.

"You boys go back to sleep. Aunt Arlene is coming over to stay with you."

Dad hustled out the door. I laid back and fell asleep. When I awoke, I heard Arlene's voice in the kitchen. Norman and I jumped into our overalls. We didn't want our aunt to see us in our shorts.

Grandma was in the kitchen frying bacon and mixing pancake batter.

"Sit down and eat. No cold cereal this morning. Eat all you want."

I wondered what caused this luxury. And where were Mom and

Dad?

The phone rang, and Grandma hurried to answer it. "I'll tell them."

She smiled and said, "Boys, you have a baby sister."

What? A sister? In this house? As far back as I could remember it had always been just us four boys. Now what's going to happen? What changes would take place?

Grandma said, "This is our first granddaughter. Been all boys so far."

I guessed she was right. All of our cousins on the Washburn side were boys.

Then Grandma said, "Her name is Elaine Maxine. She's named after your Aunt Elaine who died young from a throat infection."

I remembered her picture. But eating a full breakfast and thinking about a new sister occupied my mind.

Arlene told us, "You boys be good and I'll fix you wiener schnitzels for dinner."

"How about a wienerwurst?" Norman asked.

"You're a wienie," I told him.

We looked at each other until he grinned. I ran. He chased me around the table, but Arlene grabbed him. She sat us down and said she had a story to tell.

"In our family, there was a time when money ran dry. When your grandpa brought home a new breakfast cereal called CheeriOats he made up a way to save milk money. He poured milk and the cereal into a bowl. He told us to eat the cereal with a fork. When we were done, we were supposed to pass the bowl of milk to the next kid in line. That way he saved on milk."

We sat and stared at her.

"Don't tell our Dad. He'll make us eat that way."

"Is that the truth?"

"You don't look skinny."

Arlene laughed and then Kenny asked, "When's Mom coming home?"

"She's in the hospital for a week. Your Dad will be home this afternoon."

So it happened. Each of us had to print a letter to Mom. A baby crib appeared next to Mom's bed. Our other Grandma, Grandma Russell, came and stayed with us a few days. Then one day Mom was home and glad to see us. A baby stayed covered up in the crib. Nothing exciting happened, so my brothers and I continued our disruptive behavior and grew taller.

I could tell the baby girl would never be spanked. Mom was extremely happy. Sure, she loved her sons, but she had wanted a daughter. I watched my sister, but I soon realized she would never play the outdoor games my brothers and I played. Now our building held a family of seven.

In January of '49 another blizzard hit. Grandma said we got more than twenty inches of snow. We attended school whenever the two "school buses" could run on open roads. By March the snow still covered our village. By then we could buckle up our overshoes and play along the tops of the drifts. We dug tunnels to crawl in until Norman got stuck and Mom helped him get out.

Grandma sent over candy. I finally found candy which I didn't like. Boston Baked Beans just weren't sweet enough. I liked some new gum she sent. Black Jack had a licorice taste. Cloves gum had a distinctive taste, but it was sweet, so I liked it.

"Borrowed a record," Dad told us one night. "Boy howdy, it's a real humdinger. Ok boys. Listen to Spike Jones and his City Slickers play "All I Want for Christmas is My Two Front Teeth.""

That song and singer were crazy, but Dad liked it, so verdict reached. I had never heard bells and whistles coming from a record. Dad liked to listen to it so much he forgot about training us to sing it. Early April brought a twelve inch snowfall. By June small drifts lingered along fence lines.

When the weather warmed, Norman and I walked to the school house. Snow had melted and icicles as long as our arms hung down from the building. Thick at the top, they ended in sharp points, like daggers. If the sun were shining, you could see a deep frost rainbow color in them.

"Grab a stick," Norman said.

We smacked the icicles at their tops. We watched them crash to the windswept ground where they shattered with a jump and a tingle. Entertainment and amusement above splendor and grandeur was our custom.

The years '48 and '49 found us in a newer but smaller home. Dad continued to gamble and have fun with us. Mom babysat for a farm woman who taught at the Wann school for a semester. She paid Mom with fresh milk and farm eggs. All the rich milk we could drink, now that wasn't poverty. I would drink a half glass before bed. A full belly at night made me think I was in paradise.

As kids, what were we suppose to do when an event happened that caused us to freeze up inside? Never mention it, keep it to ourselves, and be scared to death when the incident happened without a warning.

I shouldn't have been surprised when Dad got into a fight with Uncle Wendell. But I was. The older I became, the more I realized that the memory of happy times could be erased when the shit hit the fan, as Dad once said.

On a typical winter's night, our family walked over to Grandpa's for a visit after supper. Just talk, a little beer sipped, and a candy treat from Grandma.

Most visits ended the same. Grandpa pulled out his wind-up toy from a closet. No matter the hardship of the day, if we could see and hear that toy before bed, then happiness went to sleep with us.

The characters from the Lil' Abner comic strip were arranged in a band. After Grandpa turned it on, a catchy song would play, the tinny characters would move to the rhythm. My favorite was the drummer. I felt like dancing a jig or at least like jumping up and down. When the music stopped we went home.

As we concentrated on the musical toy, suddenly there came a commotion out in the kitchen. Chairs knocked over, loud cuss words, but the pierce of Grandma's cry brought fear and shock to our hearts.

At the first sound, Grandma pushed past me to the kitchen door. I glanced around her to stare at Dad and Wendell. They wrestled each other down to the floor. Grandma screamed again. Grandpa added his own cuss words.

The fighters broke up but still cussed each other. Mom cried and helped us into our jackets. Our family fled the kitchen door to the outside. Dad stopped and pulled out a pulp magazine from under his arm. We watched him tear it to shreds and scatter the pieces in Grandpa's front yard.

In the moonlight we walked up the lane to the road to our brick house. I wanted to scream at Dad. Rex came barking at us. Dad didn't cuss or kick at him. Once inside the bank building, we went to bed without talking. I thought that all we had was family, but now it was ripped apart.

Our uncles, Wendell and Larry, seemed to like us. We liked any attention from them. *What would happen now,* I wondered. Being teased usually brought laughter. Being pissed off at family members usually brought shunning and relatives taking sides.

I would gladly give up all the good times if we never had a terrible time. Dad seemed extra-sensitive to being pushed around. He wasn't afraid to stand up to people; I wondered why I was.

In the early summer, Dad came home one night with exciting news.

"Listen to this. Got a chance to make a ton of money. They got three miles of railroad track on the Mead ammunition plant. They'll give it to anyone who'll move it."

"What will you do with it?" Mom asked.

"Hell, figure I can hire welders. They can cut the track into pieces we can load on trucks. Then haul them to a scrap metal yard in Omaha. Make a killing."

We listened to him talk on the phone. Any amount of money meant good things for us. However, I had taken to heart one of Grandma's favorite sayings—"Don't count your chickens before they hatch." Dad came home the next night in a foul mood.

"Damn them. Railroad won't deal with us. They want a big company to come in and clean it up fast. The horsesasses."

This was not happy news. The next day Dad had to take us to Lincoln for new shoes. The ordeal was dreadful enough without him being in a bad mood.

"Hurry up," he said, "can't feed you in Lincoln. Got to be back here for lunch."

We grabbed a piece of buttered toast with strawberry jam. The ride was quiet since we knew what would happen. He was never happy to waste money on shoes which we didn't take care of. He inserted cardboard in the bottoms if we wore a hole in them.

In the summer if our toes pinched, Dad would cut out the top of the shoe so our toes hung over the edge. At night we would take them off outside to shake the sand out. A few times one of us outgrew a decent pair. Then the next in line would inherit those and not get a new pair.

After the trip to Lincoln, Dad parked on O Street, the main street of the city.

"Get in the store and down to the basement."

We walked down the stairs in the Wells and Frost shoe store and sat down.

Dad asked the salesman, "Got anything on sale?"

The salesman brought out boxes for us.

Dad leaned over to Norman and me, "Hide those holes in your socks, dammit. Don't let him see those."

If it weren't for Dad's grim humor, it might have been fun. Beginning with Norman, we inserted our feet into an x-ray machine. At the top there were three eye holders. We saw our toe bones. Dad looked at the size. The salesman used a pointer stick to show Dad where there was plenty of room for our feet to grow into.

When I got up, the salesman said, "There a problem with his left foot? Looks smaller."

"He was born that way. Don't try to sell me two pair for him. Size the right foot, I'll take care of the rest. Let's see how much discount you're giving since I'm buying four pair."

I didn't need two pair to take care of anyway. Dad supplied me with cardboard pieces which I inserted behind my left heel. One or two and then the shoe felt snug.

If Dad couldn't bully a particular salesman, he would drive home mad. At least the ordeal was over for another year. We wore our brown shoes to school, to play in, and for chores. On Sundays we brushed brown liquid over them to cover the scuff marks.

One fall morning Mickey came running into the house.

"Worms. Lots of worms."

We ran with him to the backyard. Next to the shed was a sorry-looking elm tree which didn't grow straight. Mick pointed to a place above our heads. We stared at hundreds of worms in motion inside a sagging web. The sight made me sick to my gut. There were three of the scary webs. We ran back to get Dad.

"Get shovels and boards."

We grabbed what we could see. Dad came out with rolled up newspapers.

"Want you boys to smash them when they fall to the ground."

He lit the papers on fire and held them under the first web. The smoke and flames circled the web. The worms increased their frantic activity. I stood back.

The flames burned a hole in the bottom of the web, and the worms began to fall.

"Kill 'em, kill 'em."

We smashed our boards down on the mass. I kept my feet back, didn't want anything crawling up my legs. Dad went in as soon as the three webs fell. We backed off to watch our flock of Banty chickens move in for a feast. I knew for damn sure what one dream would be about that night.

It was just another episode for the family to survive. I followed Norman through the grades at the stone school building. Mom talked how she would like to move to Ashland since this building didn't have enough space. I watched Dad for his happy moods so the family would be happy for a time.

One morning Dad woke us up with a surprise.

"Come on boys. Here's a new cereal for you. Called Rice Krispies. Pour milk on them. Listen to them snap, crackle, and pop."

We leaned down to hear after we poured the milk. Once again magic excited us.

"I want another bowl."

"Norman got more than me."

"Did not."

"One bowl apiece. If I heard any more whining nobody gets any more."

The next day Dad announced, "Your Grandpa butchered a cow. We're gonna eat fresh meat."

That night he brought home three packages. Mom opened the first one and boiled the meat. When I saw the grey steaming tongue, I almost barfed. No way in hell would I put that in my mouth. Dad cut pieces and put them on our plates.

"Try this or get the yardstick."

I could be starving to death and still wouldn't eat that mess. I ate a piece of bread while cutting my slice in half. I slid my portions to Jigger who sat by me. Later I snuck a couple of saltine crackers and went to bed only a little hungry.

The next morning Mom opened the second package.

"Try these calf brains. I fried them and scrambled eggs."

I could eat the eggs, but the brains looked like hash brown potatoes. I put a helping in my mouth with the eggs and got my piece down. Tried not to think about it being in the calf's head.

For supper Mom fried the meat from the last package. The odor coming from the kitchen was delicious, so I went to look.

"What's that?"

"It's heart. Tastes just like steak. Think you'll like it."

And I did. I grabbed the last extra bit. An argument began so Dad laid the yardstick on the table. We shut up. My insides felt extended that night when I went to bed. Later we would eat heart again but never brains or tongue.

Since entertainment was hard to come by in Wann, we had to fool around and create fun things to do. When Dad was gone, we studied the wooden wall telephone. To reach the operator, we had to push a button on one side and turn a hand crank on the other.

Norman invented a game since the Washburn boys weren't satisfied with something common. He told us we needed to see who could "take the pain."

If we operated the button and the crank just so, our finger pushing the button would register a mild electric shock. We took turns raising hell with that phone. Sometimes it quit working and then we listened to Dad cuss up a blue streak.

CHAPTER SEVEN

August, 1989

On my way home from a visit with Dad and Mom, A rough memory overwhelmed me. We became used to Dad's leaving and returning. But one day Mom left us.

1949

I walked away from our cramped house to think about why I wanted more independence from Dad, yet still wanted his approval. I wondered why the bust times were more frequent, but the boom times carried more weight. In-between there were days of uncomplicated pleasures. Security for me came from the sameness of many days.
 The sun was out most summer days. The fluffy, mashed-potato clouds floated in a blue sky. The smell of fresh green grass in April was better than the smell of beer. There was the strangeness of an old stink in a pile of manure behind Grandpa's red barn.
 A farm girl catching polio shattered the calmness. A farm boy dying in his bed from a horse accident affected our hearts. Another one of Dad's money schemes would provoke laughter if he weren't listening.
 At Sunday school, I learned the Psalm which taught that our lives are like a short hour in the night, and we last no longer than a dream. But the family had lasted so far, why couldn't we keep surviving? However, no matter how hard I tried, I couldn't see ahead.
 When I turned eight, a sense of rebellion slowly grew in me. I felt a desire for something in my future that was different from Dad's life style. My main worry after Easter was why Mom left us and never said goodbye. I had experienced a variety of pains before, but this was the worst.
 We were just simple-minded kids, so how were we supposed to know why she left? I walked home from the fourth grade one afternoon to see Norman stumble out of our house and announce, "Mom's gone."

"Where to?"

I kept my distance, not grabbing his arms with fear since our family never touched, never. Except with the yardstick or belt.

"Don't know."

Norman glanced down. On the cement slab sat a green paint-peeling icebox with one door hanging by a hinge, a red feed barrel, a galvanized wash tub standing on four crooked legs and a baby stroller with two wheels missing. Norman's announcement ended the bounce in my walk.

"Where, dammit?"

Ignoring the tears in his eyes, I pushed past him toward the door. Growing up, I thought it was fun to cuss and swear. Besides, other kids did it, and we thought it was common.

I pulled open the rickety screen door, caught a whiff of kerosene from the heater and looked in. Dad looked pissed off. He stood in the kitchen stirring a pan of tomato soup. He wore his usual white shirt and faded blue slacks.

Him and his gambling, I thought. He's the reason she's gone was the quickest notion which entered my mind. He gave me a look that said keep my mouth shut. Dad had large hands and arms, and his light-colored hair was beginning to thin out.

The whistle from the Puddle Jumper train took my mind off the news. I sneaked a peek at the short train until it disappeared behind a line of stationary boxcars. My gut felt queasy. The kerosene and soup aroma mixed with the feeling of abandonment made it hurt like hell.

I escaped to take my mind off Mom. I pulled our red wagon to the side of our house. There was no grass or weeds, just loose sand which spread out into the road. I held the handle then placed a knee inside the wagon. I pushed with my other foot, made a path. It was a long figure eight which I pretended was a bus route.

I followed the route repeatedly. I was a bus driver then a train engineer then a truck driver. Finally, I didn't know who I was. Dad called for supper, but I ignored him. I wheeled, I pushed, I did everything I could to take my mind off Mom. Then Dad grabbed my arm and hauled me in.

When you opened the front screen, you could see the entire inside: The ragged-edged linoleum, the icebox, the wooden table and chairs, and the heater. Straight back was a small kitchen and back to the right were two beds. There was an outhouse, but if no one were watching, we snuck behind a tree to take a leak.

"Where's Mom?"

I spied Mickey and Kenny at the table. Maybe it was a miracle Mom survived eleven years of marriage. Always scrounging for money, trying to raise four wild-horse boys, and at times darned little food to cook. You would think we were living in the depression of the '30s, but this was 1949.

This woman had frequent reasons to shed tears. Her four sons were to blame as much as anyone. We were sickly, lazy, and did stupid things like eating X-Lax because it tasted like candy. She worked as she was expected to do. She emptied and cleaned the slop bucket, scrubbed clothes on a washboard, ironed all our clothes, darned socks, scrubbed the floors, killed and plucked chickens and cooked every meal.

Mom wrote this in her diary six months after I was born. "I'm so hungry. We don't have a thing to eat. I'm afraid my little boys are starving. They're crying so hard. Oh dear Lord, what are we going to do?"

Mom told us Dad had gambled before they married. Getting married and having kids didn't change his habits. Ken looked at me and shrugged his shoulders. Just like me, afraid to say much in Dad's presence.

"She's in Omaha for a while, so you can all quit your damn whining," Dad said as he plopped the pan of soup on the table. Norman and I pulled up our chairs and sat. Dad doing household chores was something different.

"What for?"

I couldn't let it rest. I was starting to figure out some things on my own. I felt ashamed at school not knowing what to fill in on a card where it asked "father's occupation."

"I said 'shut up' or I'll give you something to whine about."

Watery tomato soup with no crackers was better than nothing. We learned to eat slowly to make food items last. Unless there were six pieces of fried chicken feet. Then the first two finished could grab the last two feet. That's the way it was and no questions asked. If we tried hard enough, we could find some meat on a chicken foot.

"Two oldest wash and wipe the dishes."

Being our usual chore we got to it after we carried in water. My usual jealous thought was why the two little fartnhammers didn't have to do any work.

The April rain kept us inside. Dad wouldn't turn on the radio. We didn't have a TV yet. I wondered how we could survive without the mother who fed, cleaned, and clothed us. Dad wasn't even playing his favorite Little Jimmy Dickens record.

Later that evening Dad sat studying the Daily Racing Form. The screen door opened and Grandma pushed in carrying a box. We were sorting out our collection of pop bottle caps, great toys in the absence of the real things.

"Wha'cha going do with them?" She asked Dad.

I wanted to rush her for a hug to regain stability, but I sat still. We learned that independent actions weren't tolerated. I hid my feelings until sleep helped me forget about them.

"Step outside."

Dad motioned to her. So, the relatives knew, and now the whole damn village would know. Truth be told—everyone rubbered in on the telephone party line.

What about the Wann Ladies Aid busybodies gathering and spreading the news? Nothing takes a trip quicker than small-town gossip. It's easier to stop the snow in the winter than to get the Ladies Aid women to shut up.

Norman looked in the box. "Look, four sack lunches with an orange and a sandwich."

"Think they're for us?"

Joy upon joy, for one day we could be like the farm kids who brought their lunches in Karo Syrup cans with wire handles. We always had to walk home to eat. A real sack lunch took the bite out of going to bed without Mom.

Norman and I unfolded the lumpy couch, placed a sheet, blanket, and two pillows on it. Our "bed" extended next to the table. I felt sick as I tried to fall asleep. What we needed was a real Joe Palooka, or a genuine Steve Canyon to fight off dreams of Germans and Japs overflowing our hamlet. Where the heck was Dick Tracy when we needed him?

The next morning brought the usual, a bowl of cold cereal with milk. *It's better than poached eggs,* I thought. Then Dad surprised us.

"Leave the lunches here."

"Why?"

I couldn't control my disappointment or my mouth.

SLAP! It was nothing, just a blow to my shoulder. It knocked me off balance for a second.

"Cause I said so, that's why." He towered over me. "You guys come home for lunch and share with me."

Right then I quit looking forward to anything good. I knew damn well he'd ruin it. I thought about crying to Grandma, but that would get me into worse trouble.

I emptied the remaining Wheaties into my bowl. "It's my turn for the gorilla mask."

"No, it's mine." Norman said. "You got the last one, the Lone Ranger."

"The heck I did."

"Shut up, the both of you." Dad grabbed the box from me and sat down holding a pair of scissors. "Take your shoes off."

Dad cut the Wheaties box top, the sides, and the mask into oval-sized shapes. He placed the cardboard in the bottom of our shoes. I was pissed I didn't get the mask, but my disposition was such that it was a victory over Norman; he didn't get the mask either.

There was another day of memorization and recess at school. At noon we walked home to our sack lunch. I ate my share, kept my mouth shut, and then hiked back to school.

A few guys stood by the storm cellar. Wayne Nast came up and said, "Hey, heard your family busted up. What's wrong with you guys?"

"Shut up, you son-of-a-bitch."

Wayne wrestled me down and sat on my chest. He tried to slug my face, but I was too fast. He let me up when the bell rang. I called him a horse's ass and then ran for the classroom.

When Miss Barta wasn't looking, I reached inside my desk for my Smith Brothers Cough Drops. I had convinced Mom I needed them for my throat. The strong taste of the black drops was a candy treat. Not supposed to have candy during school, but I was improving on my sneakiness.

Grandpa came over before supper. "Here's three dollars for gas. Go get her."

"Come out here." Dad picked up the racing form and pulled Grandpa outside. I heard him say, "Look, here's a sure thing. Can you spare five more dollars? Pay you back tomorrow night."

For supper, Dad said he had a surprise. He handed a plate and fork to each. He opened a box of saltine crackers and placed four on each plate. Then he pulled out a package of raw hamburger.

"This is called a tiger meat sandwich. Now watch."

He placed a pile of raw hamburger on one cracker. He shook salt and pepper on the meat. He positioned another cracker on top and began to chew.

"Go ahead. Try it."

If Mom were home, we would be eating one of her home-cooked meals, maybe fried chicken or hamburger gravy on a slice of bread. I forced down one tiger sandwich and then I ate the last two crackers without meat.

"Boys, I'm going to bet on a winner tomorrow and bring your mom home. Now, take your shirts off. Sit your butts on the back of this chair."

Oh no, haircut time. He didn't put a cereal bowl on our heads, but the result made us look like hicks, like hillbillies. His hand-operated clippers pinched the hairs out of our scalps. If the pain caused us to snivel he called us crybabies.

Since he was in a good mood, he played one of his favorite records, "The Tennessee Waltz" by Patti Page. I didn't want to hear a sad song. Then he played one of my favorites, but I wouldn't tell him that. "Ghost Riders in the Sky".

He called Norman and me to the table. He laid the yardstick down. Then he has us read a page in the racing form.

"Norman. Who won the third race?"

"Clems Lark."

"What weight did he carry and what was his post position?"

"One hundred eighteen pounds and in the third gate."

"Warren. Who was the jockey?"

"Rettele."

"How much did he pay to win?"

"Five dollars and eighty cents."

"How much did he win by?"

"Five lengths."

"How far is a length?"

"I don't know."

"Norman. How far is a length?"

"Not too far."

Dad picked up the yardstick and slammed it down on the table.

"Boys. you learning anything at that damn school? Is all you do is chase girls? Tomorrow find out how far a length is. Some day I might take you to the races, and I don't want a bunch of dummies running around after me."

The next day when we walked home for supper he was waiting. "Sit down. Get a piece of bread and a slice of pickled ham."

I drooped down in my chair, fearing the news, but still not able to resist setting him off. "Where's Mom?"

"One more word out of you and I'm getting the yardstick. You think you could pick a winner? Huh? Just shut up about it."

Norman did homework. I picked up a Cisco Kid comic book, and the other two played with Jigger.

Dad went to the phone, racing form in hand. He pushed the button in and held it down, and then gave the hand crank a few vigorous turns. He picked up the receiver and gave the operator a number.

"Bomber here."

"Yeah, I know, but you know I'm good for it. You'll get your money next week."

"You going to take my bet or not?"

"Okay, tomorrow at Santa Anita, second race. I want five on Little Red Man to win. That's right, and quit worrying about it."

It's never going to end, I thought.

Dad turned on the radio. Maybe we could listen to *Gunsmoke* or *Gangbusters*. But no, it was a music station. "Buttons and Bows" and then we listened to "Red Roses for a Blue Lady". Dad whistled along.

Getting ready for bed, I thought that a feeling of dread was worse than a hunger pang. I thought how he had lost Grandpa's money on his "sure thing." He hadn't paid the ten dollar monthly rent, but he was still trying to pick a winner. However, before bed it was time again for homework.

"What does Ak-Sar-Ben stand for?" Dad asked after he made us sit at the table.

I was quick with the answer. "Nebraska, spelled backwards."

"Norman, what's the best five card poker hand with no pairs?"

"Ace high, then king, then queen."

"What's the next best hand?" It was my turn.
"A pair of anything."
"What'll beat a pair?"
"Three of a kind?"
"Oh yeah, what about a straight or a flush?"
We didn't know.
"Boys, what's a flush, and you had better know."

Neither of us knew. Norman was showing an interest in girls, and I had my head in Bobbsey Twins and Tarzan books. If we were spanked for not knowing what a flush was, we figured the world was unfair.

"Maybe you boys can learn something about horse races. Here's a program from Santa Anita. Who's the jockey on Wingover?"

"Willie Hartack." I was sure I got that right after reading the program.

"Who's the trainer?"
"Hurst Philpot."
"What's a maiden colt?"
We didn't know.
"What's a gelding?"
I ventured, "A male goose?"
"Hell no!"
"Norman, what's the purse?"
"Four thousand."
"Okay, go to bed. One last one, where's Santa Anita?"
"Mexico?" Norman guessed.

"Oh, hell, hell and damnation," Dad sputtered. "Might as well not send you to school. Ain't learning a damn thing."

The next morning he said, "Get your jackets. Don't go to school."

He put on his gray hat. We watched as he walked the two blocks to Grandpa's to borrow more money. On a misty, gray morning, we trooped out to his Chevy. He stopped at the general store to pump in a few gallons of regular gas. Then off we went on the muddy roads to Omaha.

"Dammit, dammit," he cried as the car slid sideways into a mud-spattered ditch. We had driven four miles.

The steering wheel had locked up. Thirty minutes later, after Old Man Larson had pulled us home, Dad told him, "I'll get you a winner at Ak-Sar-Ben next week."

"Car broke down, maybe come and get you tomorrow." We heard him say into the phone.

"You boys stay home till noon. Then go back to school."

I could tell he handled problems by getting pissed off. I had discovered a little secret. I would clam up until I could "take his temperature". If he won money we could be happy—laugh, raise hell in our words and actions, and have coins for candy and soda pop.

However, if he lost he'd stomp in and cuss because someone used or lost his lucky pen, or left a hat on a bed, or opened an umbrella indoors. These were all bad luck omens, and someone should catch hell. Either Mom or we had jinxed him. Get out of the house then was our best bet. He used the word "jinx" quite a bit.

Dad was after-the-fact superstitious. Of course, a bird getting into anyone's house was a direct warning of a death. It could mean a family death in the past or foretelling one upcoming. Mom and Aunt Arlene appeared scared once because a sparrow flew into our house.

Another day of not paying attention at school, but when we came home there was Mom in her flowered house dress. She was standing with her back to us, leaning against the icebox, and crying. We stood slack-kneed, with mouths open, afraid to say anything. Then I noticed the floor of the kitchen. It was so black with mud you couldn't see the linoleum. I guessed we had been living like pigs.

After a few minutes, she recovered and said, "Norman, go out and catch an old hen. I'm going to fry chicken for supper."

She fired up the kitchen stove and began to heat water. Mom's fried chicken, I thought. How could any meal be better than that?

I watched Norman grab a broom from the shed. We chased a white hen around until she tired out and squatted by the elm tree. We grabbed her and fought off her flapping wings.

I held the hen down with one hand and stretched out her neck with the other. Norman laid the broom handle across her neck and then stepped on it, one foot on each side. I let go, stood up, and moved away. He grabbed the hen's feet and gave them a backward jerk. The body separated from the neck, and then he gave it a toss.

We watched the headless body shake, kick, and spurt blood. Mom appeared with a pail of scalding water. She held the chicken by its feet and dipped it up and down in the hot water. We pulled the feathers off and scattered them in the yard.

It was the little brothers' turn to eat the chicken feet, so they benefitted from additional meat. I got an extra piece since no one wanted the neck. Before bedtime Mom mixed hot lemonade with baking soda so our drink fizzed at the top of a glass. For the first time in a week, I could go to bed without alarm. I could relax and forget about the kerosene smell.

Saturday morning Dad got a call after eating his two poached eggs. Little Red Man had run second, now he owed more. The house grew still as he slammed the door. He returned in the late afternoon.

"Get your jackets. We're going to town. I hit a lick!"

He had driven to the bookies in Omaha and won enough to pay his bills and more.

"Here boys, a quarter for each for the picture show."

Mom got ten dollars for groceries. A week of nightmares erased with one winning bet. We lived seven miles from paradise. We would be in the Ashland town for a Saturday night hullabaloo with twenty-five cents to spend.

God sends down his tender mercies on the good and the bad, I thought.

Mom asked, "Are we eating supper in town?"

"Yup. Everyone gets a hamburger at the Silver Café."

Dad borrowed Grandpa's panel truck which had two seats up front. We sat on planks which rested on two cement blocks. We didn't care if it were a bumpy ride; we were headed toward Entertainment City.

Just think--Ashland on a warm spring night. Silver Street crowded with cars. Sidewalks full of people, clusters out in front of the Chambers Hardware store watching the black and white TV through the window, beer joints billowing out the smoke of cigarettes and sweet beer smell, the sound of smacking snooker balls, carry-out boys hauling sacks from Harold's Grocery, the farm wife stocking up for another week's food supply. The farmers had flocked in earlier to do their trading; cashing in their eggs, milk, and cream at the Ashland Creamery located near the railroad depot.

My brothers and I had never eaten in a cafe. We kept quiet as Dad squeezed the seven of us into a large booth. We sat shoulder to shoulder but never shoved or complained. Dad ordered, we ate and were eager to leave since we weren't sure how to act when eating with strangers.

Now to spend the quarter. Taking home any change was as foreign to us as China. We lived for the moment, and when the boom time hit, we knew what to do. First, the picture show--western, sci fi, gangsters, Fred Astaire tap dancing—we didn't care; magic was on the screen. I sat with my two younger brothers and Dude Vosler, a classmate from Wann.

Dude lived on a ranch two miles from Wann. He wore blue jeans, a cowboy belt and cowboy boots. He would rather move through space on a horse than run like my brothers and me.

Norman hung back, talking to older boys, and looking at giggling girls. I glanced at them, but girls were more than I wanted to think about at my age. I could see couples snuggling in the dark at the back of the theater.

Admission to the show was thirteen cents, and we got a bargain. First, a black and white news reel. War news, political news, sports news, we didn't care. Next, a cartoon. Mighty Mouse was my favorite. Sometimes kids in the audience would cheer when Mighty Mouse made his appearance.

Before the main attraction, there was a preview. I thought someone was trying to fool us. The preview said there would be a double-feature on the following weekend. Even if this were true, I figured the manager would charge double which meant a quarter wouldn't be enough.

No matter what was on the screen I sat there tense and quiet. The show was Ma and Pa Kettle on a farm. I wanted to laugh at times, but I didn't see too much funny about poor people and Pa acting stupid.

After the movie, I cried, "Come on, Dude, let's go."

I hustled across the main street trying to ditch my little brothers. They could go find Mom; I wanted some independence. Norman hung out with guys who talked to girls.

Dude and I ran up to the old ladies' popcorn stand. She was cranky and scolded us in a foreign language if we complained, but she handed out a large bag of fresh popcorn for five cents. She lived on the outskirts of town in an abandoned gas station with dogs and cats roaming about like a runaway pet shop.

We walked up and down the main street while we ate popcorn, taking in sights and aromas. Looking in store windows and watching people was customary for us out-of-towners from the remote villages of Wann, Memphis, Mead and Yutan.

Hoffman's IGA displayed a donut-making machine. The barbershop stayed open for fifty-cent haircuts. We squandered the last seven cents at Harris's Drugstore for penny candy. It took time to make our main decision. Some candy sold for one cent each, and some were two-for-a penny. We always went for quantity since the memory of the scarce times never left us.

I bought four cents of Root Beer Barrels at two for a penny. Then three cents worth of black Licorice Babies. Old man Harris acted pissed because he had to waste his time on pennies, but I didn't care.

Finally, Mom and Dad rounded us up. Mom had shopped for groceries and visited with friends and relatives. Dad sat in the back of the Town Tap to play poker. The drunks tired the night out, the farmers headed home in their pickups, and two cars met a mile out so guys could pass money to Skip who then gave them a six-pack of Miller High Life.

What a night! The excitement, the girls, the donut machine, the autos cruising Silver Street, the booze, the movie, the silver quarter, the old popcorn lady, the town teeming with magic moments! One Saturday night in town would wipe out lots of hard time memories. Who could ask for anything more?

The seven mile journey to Wann crossed four rusted iron bridges. The trip put us to sleep until bumps jerked our heads as the sugar candy coated our teeth.

At the end of these visits, we would fall into bed at once. Then Sunday we could do whatever we wanted. After bedtime on Sunday night, Dad allowed the family to play one of our favorite games.

He whistled a tune, and we would compete to see who could name it first. In the dark there would be his whistle and then a quick call from the first one to identify it. I would lay there in a state of tension since our family grew up on competition. I desired to beat my brothers and my Mom.

I didn't understand how Dad did it, but I wanted his approval even though at times he put us through hell. I would do something ornery at times if I thought I wasn't getting enough attention. After the whipping, I had a strange feeling that I didn't despise him since I knew I was on his mind.

Life was back to normal by Monday. The gambling man drove off for another journey on another road to another town and a different racetrack. Family life was calmer. By the end of a week-and-a-half, we were once again on emergency provisions.

Norman and I would wander over to the Wann general store before noon. Sometimes a kind truck driver delivering supplies would hand out a free sample of something. How could he resist a pair of skinny boys with hick haircuts and wearing washed-thin bib overalls? I loved to see the look on Norman's face as he ran home to Mom with a gift and a grin.

We were Wann kids once again as the Earth completed its cycles. We existed as a poor man's example of a fool's paradise. We were pitiable, hungry, impoverished in all things at times, then acted crazy and out of our ever-loving minds during the boom times. I'm positive we drove the angels crazy.

We lined up in order of birth for snapshots. Our faces, our clothes, our tricycles and bikes would show up frozen on black and white photos for all time. We weren't bothered when Dad bet on the phone or drove away. We were just simple-minded little kids. A few years later my brothers and I would be baptized in the Wann sandpits, fully immersed. God had his plan and kept the family in his tender mercies.

CHAPTER EIGHT

SEPTEMBER 1989

On my next visit I found Dad on the third floor of the nursing home. His bed was in a small room for two; an Asian man on oxygen lay in the other bed. How did Dad accept that I wondered? Dad's face showed better color. He could take himself to the bathroom by using his walker.

"Go across the street. Get me a chocolate malt."

"Sure you're supposed to have one?"

"Hell yes, I can have what I want. And when you going to get me out of here?"

"Have to see the doc about that, Dad."

I took my time getting the malt. I hoped he'd forget about going back to live with Mom.

Our visit lasted an hour. He told me about his time in the Civilian Conservation Corps. He helped plant trees in the Halsey National Forest in central Nebraska. From his thirty dollar monthly wage, he could keep five. The remainder mailed home to his folks.

"Dad, what can you remember about living in Wann?"

"Shack was all I could afford. You had that damn club foot. Doctor fixed it for free. Had bad luck at the races."

"Do you remember the time you tried to make money with a chain letter?"

He wouldn't talk about his money-making schemes, his rabbit pens.

1950

My brothers and I were destined to catch any childhood disease which appeared in Wann. Chicken pox felt the worst. There was nothing to do but sit around and suffer from the itching. When I couldn't stand it any longer, I would scratch my blisters like crazy then suffer from worse itching.

After we had healed, Aunt Joann paid a visit on a cold afternoon. She taught Norman and me how to play Uncle Wiggly. She told us that once we learned that game she would teach us Monopoly.

A car horn sounded. Mom opened the door. She turned and said, "Get your coats. Come on."

We bundled up, ran out the door and then stopped and stared. Dad sat in the driver's seat of a newer car. His hat, tilted back on his head, caused his bald forehead to show.

The car was a used '46 Ford, two-door coupe V8. It was shiny black with a large hood and balloon tires. We ran and shoved to be the first to jump in.

"Dammit boys, knock the snow off your shoes. Want to keep this baby looking good for a long time."

Mom, Elaine, and our aunt climbed in the front seat and off we flew. Dad drove fast on the country roads to Ashland. He drove up and down Silver Street. We looked to see if anyone stared at the car. I forgot about my motion sickness.

After we had driven back to Wann, Dad let our aunt out at Grandpa's lane. We gathered around to hear his story.

"Won a bunch in a poker game at the Town Tap. Got a hot tip for Hot Springs. Bet the whole bundle and won. Put a down payment on the car."

Once the word spread, the Chevy kids at school became belligerent. They argued which was the best, Chevys or Fords. Even the farm girls chimed in. They just repeated what their parents said. Some kids almost got into fights.

A nicer car had never been seen in Wann. But still, we lived in a small house and had to use an outdoor toilet. Using it wasn't too bad if there was a roll of toilet paper inside.

The worst times were when the Sears & Roebuck catalog pages took the place of the regular roll. Damn, when those pages crinkled up they gave me cuts in my butt. Aunt Aloha told us about farm families using corncobs, but we never used them.

Once when Dad and Mom were out I had a sudden craving for chocolate. Usually I would feel that way in the general store. I would stare inside the candy counter and wish. Seldom would a nickel's worth of luck visit my way.

I walked to the kitchen. I knew that in a top cabinet there was a little red box of X-Lax. I knew what it was for, but I thought that a little bite wouldn't affect me.

"Norm, want a bite?"

He was smarter and shook his head. I pushed a chair over to the counter. I reached into the cabinet, grabbed the X-Lax box and savored a little nibble. I loved that bitter chocolate tang. Quickly, I wrapped the remaining bar, returned the box, and secured the cabinet door. Then I felt I couldn't resist.

Twice more I repeated the action. Mom came home and fixed fried potatoes. I felt okay until an hour later. Then my stomach felt like it was percolating. I told Mom I felt sick. Instead of sending me to the outhouse she sat me on a pot in the bedroom.

I felt little pain, just a lot of relief. After an hour, the bedroom stunk. Dad cussed. I didn't dare get up. Mom cleaned and emptied the pot. By the time she tucked me in bed, I felt drained, weak, and woozy. However, I did learn another life lesson.

One thing I had trouble with at school was using the outhouse. I would never raise one or two fingers to let Miss Barta know I had to go. The girls would know what I had to do. It was too embarrassing. I would hold on until we walked home for lunch. Or I would wait until after school and then run to our outhouse. Twice I didn't make it. I never used the school outhouse until I was twelve years old and in the seventh grade.

One morning we woke while it was still dark. There was a commotion outside. I heard Dad yelling. Norman and I stumbled out of bed. Mom grabbed us and held us back.

I remembered some hushed talk. "How we going to make the next payment," and "why is our luck so rotten." Dad came in and slammed the door.

"The bastards repossessed it."

"What will we do now?"

"I'll borrow Sam's car or truck. I've borrowed Fred Tarpington's car before. Have to try it again."

And that's what happened. Dad borrowed cars and money. He helped Grandpa sell eggs, tomatoes, and strawberries. We helped Sam manage his watermelon stand at the state fair in Lincoln. Dad took our share of monies and bought a Chevy clunker.

All of these events kept adding up in my mind. I knew I couldn't do anything about them, but I thought about them. I paid attention to Mom when she said, "It's a good thing that no one can see the future."

Dad wasn't stupid, but I never understood why he did things that made me distrust him.

"You two boys, back in the bedroom."

Norman and I wondered what was up. Our Aunt Arlene and Uncle Wendell were visiting. They were laughing as they usually did around Dad.

"Get your shoes off. Get on the bed. Wrestle each other. Let's see who's the toughest."

See what I mean? Norman is bigger, stronger, and older. What the hell. I knew the outcome but decided I would go down fighting.

Norman was good-natured, so I tried to dance around him. Soon he started to laugh so I grabbed his leg and pulled him down.

Dad cried out, "He looks like a banty rooster."

Norman decided he had had enough, so he rolled over on top and held me down. I struggled, and my face became flushed. Tears came to my eyes.

The adults laughed and clapped. Dad made Norman let me up. I wasn't mad that Norman beat me. But I thought, *what kind of person was Dad? What were we? His trained monkeys?*

As time advanced, instead of desiring his attention, I most wanted him to leave me alone. Nothing good was coming from a close association with him. Sure, he had his moments. But I knew damn well sooner or later he would lose his temper.

The next month he announced his plan to have his boys become performers. On one wall, he hung a picture of an Indian woman. She was colorfully dressed in a red and blue robe, sitting on a rock looking at the moonlight on a peaceful lake. Dad told us her name was Redwing.

"Line up here boys. Norman you're first. Now hold your right arm and hand out. Point them toward Redwing."

It seemed like a Nazi salute.

"Sing it out boys. Oh, the moon shines tonight on pretty Redwing, her heart is sighing…"

He made us memorize three verses. Then when his family came for a visit, we had to perform. They loved it. I hated it and never sang loud, just mouthed the words. A small rebellion on my part.

More than once Mom had to heat the cocoa butter for my foot. I asked her why someone had to keep doing this.

"Well," she said, "I had a hard time carrying you. Once the doctor said that I was in danger of losing my baby. And your delivery was hard. I was alone when you were born. Your dad and grandma were upset since you were handicapped."

"What was wrong?"

"You were born with a crippled foot. Some called it a clubfoot. It looked terrible. A Lincoln doctor put a cast on to straighten it out. It's okay now. It's just a little shorter than your other one. The doctor told us to massage it to help the circulation."

Sometimes the foot hurt, but in our everyday life, there were other things that were more serious. Staying warm in the winter, some food everyday and play, play, play. Getting through days like that with no disturbing dreams, then I was satisfied.

I knew that sometime in the future Thanksgiving and Christmas were coming. There would be extra food and a couple of toys apiece. How could we complain about life when our expectations were limited, and the events of the world weren't any of our business?

Dad always told us, "Keep your nose out of other people's business."

Once the school kids got into an argument about something called a UFO. That night at Grandma's I asked, "What's a UFO?"

Wendell said, "It's a real thing. It crashed in New Mexico."

Grandpa said, "The government says no. They're just covering it up. Can't trust them any further than you can throw 'em."

Wendell replied, "A guy in the snooker hall just came from there. Area all fenced. Air Force won't let anyone in. But he knew someone who took pictures and got arrested."

Dad ended it. "It's all a bunch of bullshit. Ain't no such thing as a UFO. They just got it in the news to take our minds off a Negro playing major league baseball, that's all. Nothing but a whole lot of rigmarole."

Wendell snorted, "Believe what you want. Not only do they have a UFO, there was a dead alien in it. Air Force got it on ice."

"Hold on," Dad said, "remember that story back in '44 or '45? The Japs sent exploding fire balloons across the ocean. Story got out how one came down in Omaha. A man said he saw it hit a hog shed and explode. Just a bunch of bullshit. Probably same man who saw the UFO."

Wendell slammed the screen door. I wished I had never asked the question. And I still didn't know what a UFO was.

Other things Dad did made me want to cry. I didn't understand why he did them. So what if he grew up with teasing and laughing as a method of handling the depression. He didn't have to be cruel to us, did he?

We played inside after supper in the cold times. We played with broken tinker toys, wooden spinning tops, or soda bottle caps. I could make a war battlefield out of any room.

"Listen to this, boys." He would sing softly, watching us until Mom made him stop.

"Beat the drum slowly, play the fife lowly, for I'm a young cowboy and I know I've done wrong."

I tried to hide my ears with my hands. I would think of something else. I knew he wanted to make us cry, but I'd be damned if I would give him that satisfaction.

"Play the death march as you carry me along. Take me to the green valley, lay the sod over me."

"Stop, stop," one of us cried out.

"Beat the drum slowly, play the fife lowly."

Mom made him stop. He put his hat on and walked over to his parents.

Those nights I thought about Dad dressed up in a suit, tie, and hat. We had to wear bib overalls with holes in the knees or else with large, dark-colored patches. He had a nice suit. We lived in a building framed by crumbling bricks. These thoughts caused a burn in my head. I knew I wasn't old enough to stand up to him.

Early spring of the school year, a dark cloud hung over Wann. The air seemed compressed. The adults talked in whispers or looked at us and then moved out to our kitchen. There was no way I could find out what was going on. Maybe another Shivaree, maybe Wann booted the Arkansas Shultz family out of town.

A few days earlier Norman and I had climbed over the neighbor's fence to pick and eat a couple of their apples. The housewife caught us. I didn't think Mom knew about it.

I was in the fourth grade in the little room. My favorite, Miss Barta, was the teacher. Once, when I wasn't paying attention, she had to slap me, caused my nose to bleed. I didn't lay any blame on her. Norman was in the sixth grade in the big room. He had a male teacher.

We walked home for lunch on Friday. While the sky was a pretty blue, I felt something worrying in the air. Grandma and Aunt Arlene had been visiting. They looked at us and then told Mom goodbye. Mom was quiet most of the lunch. She walked us outside and watched us walk back to school.

After the afternoon recess, we heard people walking in the hall between the two rooms. Miss Barta stuck her head out and talked for a minute. The tough look on her face told us distressing news. Then, not with any joy in her voice, she said, "Put your books away. School is out early today. The buses are here. If you live in Wann walk home."

There was a buzz in the room. Certainly this should be a cause for celebration, school out early never happened. But Miss Barta settled us down.

"When you sit down and be quiet I will dismiss you."

Why? I wondered. *What had happened? What was going to happen?* Both rooms emptied to the outside. I caught up with Norman. Then I saw what was wrong. Besides the two school buses, there were five more cars. Some men stood there watching us. Maybe they were parents of the farm kids.

We walked close to the cars.

"Look at that black one, Norm. Does it say County Sheriff on the door?"

"Yep."

I stared at that black car. When I turned around, Norman was halfway home. *What's up with him*, I thought.

There were more relatives seated around our table when I walked into our house. I heard Norman and Mom out in the kitchen having a discussion. No one offered an explanation. I heard cars drive past. Looked out the door and saw that the black car was last. Two men sat up front, and one sat in the back.

The only thing I managed to gather from the hushed discussions was that Norman's room would have a new teacher next week. Also, I heard someone say, "sick in the head," but I had no clue who they were talking about. I jumped up and down on one leg in front of Mom, but she just shook her head.

I followed Norman back to the shed after supper. He kicked at three of our Banty chickens that were scratching by the door.

"Is that right, Norm? You getting a new teacher?"

After a while he muttered, "Guess so."

"What happened to your old teacher?"

Norman sat on the step to the shed. He kept his head down. "Guess the sheriff took him."

What the hell is going on? My brain was on fire to know something. I wanted to be on the knowing side of any secrets. Norman didn't offer anything else.

I wanted to figure out what caused the uproar. I thought about how the guys at school talked about girls. The discussions were fascinating, but my thoughts tended toward football, baseball, and reading books.

Sometimes I looked at the seventh and eighth grade girls and knew they were different from the girls in my class. They were growing and budding out. Finally, I thought I had put two and two together.

I could tell Norman didn't want to talk about it, but I had to know.

"Norm, was your teacher messing with the girls?"

"No."

After saying that, Norman got up and walked out to the road toward the school.

"What then? What happened?"

I hurried after him, but it was growing dark and I couldn't see his face. He said it softly as he walked away, but I'm sure I heard correctly.

"Messing with boys."

Shocked, I stood still. My brother started jogging down the road toward our old shack. I decided to leave him alone. I glanced over to the cement storm cellar on the school ground. Older boys would catch girls and take them down there. I knew Norman participated. I never wanted to know what went on. Mosquitoes began to bite my arms, so I walked home.

As we lay on our couch that night, I was burning to ask him the ultimate question. Instead, I thought about my teacher, Miss Barta. I resolved to stop showing off in front of her, then she wouldn't have to slap me. I liked her a lot.

Norman had a pleasant woman teacher the rest of that year. The next year I moved into the big room, fifth grade. There was a new teacher, Mr. Alan Lewis. He was an outstanding teacher. Everyone who graduated from Wann and entered a nearby high school was well-prepared. He was my favorite teacher, right after Miss Barta, of course.

CHAPTER NINE

OCTOBER 1989

I hadn't seen Dad for two weeks when Mom called late at night.
"They rushed Harry to the hospital. You better come."
"What's wrong?"
"Not sure. Maybe a lung collapsed. He's in the operating room now. Can you get here?"
"Got to get off work for tomorrow. I'll be there as early as I can. Bryan Memorial?"
"Yes. Kenny's coming from Iowa."
That's the hospital where Mom had her five kids. The long drive lets me think back to how our family life gradually improved. I found the hospital and walked up to the third floor.
"How you feeling Dad?"
He was sitting up in bed. He looked weaker than before. He didn't say anything, just pointed to his stomach.
Mom said, "Something's wrong with his chest and lungs. He's not supposed to eat or drink anything."
"What was the operation for?"
"They inserted a tube in his stomach."
Dad sat staring straight ahead. Mom and I walked out into the hall.
"How does he get water if he can't drink?"
"They're inserting an IV in his hand."
"Is this for the rest of his life?"
"Guess so. Doctor said he's at risk now since his body is so weak."
Kenny appeared. We visited for a few minutes until "Warren, get in here." All of us followed Dad's command.
"Watch this," he said.
A nurse placed a funnel in his stomach tube. Then she poured a large glass of milky liquid, like a thin milk shake, into it.
Dad managed a brief smile. "Guess I'm not hungry anymore."
He closed his eyes a few minutes later. I asked Mom if he were here for good. She said they would move him back to the home if he gains strength. Kenny and I talked and then I drove home.
I asked Kenny if he remembered Aunt Jemima coming to Wann,

but he didn't. He was the youngest, so if he didn't remember all of the Wann episodes it didn't mean that my memory was faulty.

SPRING, 1950

I caught a virus in the early spring of 1950. At night my head would burn. During the day, the pain would be less, something I could live with. Reading and playing games took my mind off it.
"Mom, something's wrong. My head never quits hurting."
"Drink plenty of water."
"Do we have any medicine? Any aspirin?"
"You know better to ask. Maybe next time we're in town, I can buy some."
As time went on the nights grew worse. It seemed like my whole body was burning with infection. I couldn't help but act pissed off at everything and everyone.
This illness felt worse than the mumps, measles, or chicken pox. However, I considered I was lucky that I never caught polio, diphtheria, or scarlet fever. None of us boys ever caught the rickets. Mickey had whooping cough, but he got over it quickly.
I lay awake at night thinking how satisfying a proper bedroom would be. I thought about the icebox and wondered if I had done my chore that day. Made of wood, the icebox had tin insulation attached on the inside where a block of ice sat. The ice would melt and trickle down into a catch-all container. It was my job to empty that container once a day or else it overflowed.
At bedtime Norman and I made our bed. What kept me from sleeping was that both sections of the pull-out couch were slightly bloated in the middle.
I would help make the bed and then take off my clodhoppers and grimy socks. Next I would peel off those hated bib overalls, and then lay my sweaty body down on my section. But, if I happened to slip a bit toward the middle, my body would roll into my brother's. When that happened, I would slide back to the middle of my section. If I moved too far the other way, I would roll off the damn couch.
There I was, sleeping out in the open on an uneven piece of ratty furniture. Then, if I could maintain a balanced position, there was the problem of the uncovered light bulb to keep baby chicks warm.
How many baby chickens? Anywhere from 50 to 100. When they

started to fly out of the boxes, we took them out back. We didn't own chicken coops, so a certain amount of shrinkage had to occur. Neighborhood dogs, cars, and roosters would take their toll before the chickens were large enough to eat.

I whined around until one day, in a rush, everything cleared up. I wasn't sure how to feel normal, but I knew I never wanted to be that sick again.

That night Dad pointed at me and said, "Wash that crap off your neck."

I rubbed my hand where he pointed. Small bumps began to burn immediately. I tried to wash them off, but no luck.

Dad said, "We got to put Iodine on that."

Oh hell no. Iodine burns worse than a match. Mom painted Iodine on my neck while I gritted my teeth. The sting flared up, held its pain, and then gradually ended. I went to school with that pale pink evidence showing. Trapped in hell I was.

Three days later the bumps multiplied so the relatives came to investigate. Uncle Wendell, Grandma, and Grandpa inspected me. The Iodine treatment wasn't working.

"He's got mites. Where the hell did he catch mites?" From Grandpa.

Uncle Wendell thought it looked like ringworm. But three of us boys had ringworm the year before. The cure? That hot, stinging Iodine, of course.

"No," Grandma said, "it's the mange. Remember when our dog and a few calves caught it back in '39?"

We had a dog and chickens in the house. At times we took care of calves and hogs in the lot behind our shed. So yes, I was around animals a lot.

Uncle Wendell smiled, lit his cigarette lighter and said, "We need to burn them off."

Grandpa said, "The only way to get rid of them is to get a knife and cut them off. I mean every night."

Mom stepped up, "We'll keep putting Iodine on."

The mange spread so slowly that we measured it by the week. Next my jaw bone was covered, and then it inched up the side of my face. I hated the way school kids looked at me. After a month, it stopped growing. It began to fade away. Soon the Iodine treatments stopped. Wann was infection city as far as I was concerned.

In June, Grandpa told us that a war had started in Korea. By August, the strawberry picking had ended. Then the family pitched in to help Grandpa harvest a bumper crop of tomatoes. No one could pack a peck of tomatoes like Sam and Dad. They loaded them in Sam's panel truck and drove to Lincoln to sell to grocers.

One Saturday night Dad treated us to another new record. Gene Autry sang "Rudolph the Red-Nosed Reindeer." Dad tried to get us to memorize it, but Norman was pissed off because of a recent whipping. At times he would sing the wrong words. With a careful eye on Dad, I joined in. Mick and Ken had trouble learning the verses anyway. Dad finally gave up and started laughing.

"Damnest bunch of boys." We heard him tell Grandma. "They tried to bamboozle their old man."

Soon after, Mom fried a chicken for dinner.

"I get the neck," I said.

Norman piped up, "I want it."

Dad said, "Mick and Ken get a leg. Norman has first pick after that."

"But I called it first."

"You can have both feet if you want them. Otherwise stop you're bellyaching or you'll get nothing."

Norman said, "He can have the neck. I'll take the wishbone."

"Nope," I answered, "the wishbone is always mine and the feet."

"Shut it, the both of you or I'll take you outside." Dad said as he reached for the chicken plate. Instead, he bumped his water glass and it spilled over the table.

We sat still. If one of us spilled something, he cussed.

"Oh hell," he laughed. We laughed also but cautiously.

The phone rang then and Dad answered.

When he hung up, he told us, "Rich relatives from Lincoln driving to Wann to visit your grandparents. They're going to stop here and say hello."

We finished our chicken and bread and butter. Then we got more instructions.

"You boys wash up. Put on clean T-shirts. We'll visit with them outside. They're not coming in this house. Don't stand around and pick your nose or scratch your butt in front of them. Act like you got some manners."

We cleaned up and sat on the front cement step. We saw a

different kind of car over at Grandma's. Finally, people got in it and drove to our building. Dad and Mom, dressed up, walked out to visit.

The car seemed fancy but old. Its thin tires had spokes in them. The two women and one man sat under a black roof held up by poles on each side and in the front and back. It looked as if they were sitting in the outside air. I wondered if dust bothered them.

When Dad called us over to introduce us, we stood silent and stared at the relatives. Their names were Dot, Eva and Elmer. They didn't look like farmers or rural people; they were dressed up. Finally, Norman turned and walked back to the house, so we followed him. Back at the step, Norman produced a loud fart, then jumped up and ran around the house. We followed, all of us giggling like brainless people.

Dad must not have heard; he didn't give us hell. Later he said he was proud of everyone, we put on airs just right. "That's what you have to do when you're around rich relatives."

By this time Dad owned a better radio. Soon we had favorite programs we wouldn't miss. *Amos and Andy*, *The Jack Benny Show*, *Our Miss Brooks*, *The Lone Ranger*, and *The Charlie McCarthy Show*.

When Dad wasn't home Mom let us listen to a music station. "Goodnight Irene" and "Mona Lisa" appeared to be the station's favorites. My favorite singer was Frankie Laine. He sang "Mule Train" and "That Lucky Old Sun". That light that rolled around heaven all day.

The next week Dad planned a new method of making money. He called Grandma and Uncle Wendell to come over.

"Here's the deal. It's a chain letter. I'll make up twenty of them. Then I'll take them to Hot Springs, Arkansas, and sell them for a dollar apiece."

"Shoot," said Wendell, "twenty and a five might get you gas money and eats."

"Dammit, you don't understand how it works. I've got your name, Arlene's, Larry's and some my Ashland friends' names on it. Of course, my name is on it. I sell each letter for a dollar. Tell the buyer to send one dollar to the name on the top of the list. Then he removes that name, moves everybody up one place and puts his name at the bottom. By the time his name moves up to first he might get fifty dollars."

Grandma asked, "Is that legal?"

"Hey, I just got one like this in the mail. Don't worry. I tell the buyer to make ten copies of the new letter. Sell them for a dollar each. He's already making money. This thing could blow up big. Tell Dad he needs to stake me twenty dollars to get the ball rolling. Also, spot me this month's rent."

Wendell asked, "What about your friends? They got a chance to make a lot of money, but you do all the work."

Dad smiled. "Here's the best part. They all agreed to give me twenty percent of what they receive. Same as you, Wendell."

"Hold on. If someone sends me money, I'll be damned if I give any away."

"Ma, try to talk some sense into him, won't you?"

As Wendell stormed out, Dad yelled after him, "Are you in or out? Let me know."

Dad left the next day with Mom's blessings. She always had the highest hopes for him. He told us to start checking the mail. The dollars might be rolling in pretty quick. We were excited five days later when he drove up after supper.

"Damn hillbillies. Not smart enough to see across a room. They couldn't empty water out of a boot if the instructions were printed on the bottom."

Mom asked him how many letters he had sold, and he told her to forget about it.

I knew that he would survive one way or another. His family had a joke about calling his money schemes "rabbit pens". It would take more guts than I had to ask him, "Was this another of your rabbit pens?" Of more concern were groceries for the next meal.

During that summer, the heat lay heavy on Wann. The dogs, chickens, and us boys moved around as if we were sleep walking. When Dad's and my birthday neared, Mom thought up a special treat. We traveled to Lincoln with Dad. He went to the racetrack and Mom took us to a matinee picture show.

It was happy times like these which made us forget the outhouse, carry-in water, and the slop pail. Norman and I took turns emptying it early each morning in the garbage ditch. If necessary, we held our nose shut with one hand. Just in case someone went to the bathroom during the night.

There were two movie theaters in downtown Lincoln. We stood looking at the show posters at the first theater.

"I want to go to this one," I said.

The posters showed a giant gorilla fighting a giant snake. Other pictures showed dinosaurs chasing men through a jungle.

Norman said, "I'm not going to see that."

Kenny sided with him. I talked Mickey into going with me. Mom took Norman, Ken, and Elaine to see a western musical starring Roy Rogers and Dale Evans.

Mickey and I went to King Kong. It was an older movie making a rerun. My heart raced when Kong captured the girl and eventually chased after her.

"Norm, you should have seen King Kong. He was huge."

"Nah, movies like that give me the heebie-jeebies."

"King Kong climbed the Empire State Building."

"So what, we got to see Gabby Hayes with Roy Rogers and he's funny."

Mom took us to a drugstore for a malted milk. So, our first movie matinee and first chocolate malt all in one day. On the ride home I felt satisfied. We might run out of food, catch a disease, or be scared to death when a wind storm attacked Wann, but for one day we were in hogs' heaven.

Mom talked about a bigger house in Ashland. I wasn't worried about leaving Wann. How could our family expect anything better? Dad paid ten dollars rent per month and sometimes he missed that payment. I thought Mom should be happy we weren't living in the old shack.

In late July, I helped Norman carry a galvanized grey washtub onto the cement slab.

Norman said, "Fill the tub with water. Then wait for the sun to heat it."

While we waited, I took an empty coffee can to the back of the store. Sometimes Grandpa would empty the soda bottle caps there. I had a sizeable collection to play army with in the sandy ground of our yard. When I returned, Norman explained the contest.

"We'll take turns dunking our heads. Let's see how long we can hold our breath. I've got the kitchen clock to time us."

We held our heads under water until its coldness gave us a headache or we couldn't hold our breath any longer. Norman could do it the longest. On his last attempt, Ken became determined to last as long as Norman did.

Kenny took a couple of deep breaths, then lowered his head into the tub. After he was down for a long time, we began to cheer him on. But when his head hit the bottom of the washtub, we became worried and pulled him out.

We laid him down on the cement. He wasn't breathing. His eyeballs rolled way up. All I could see where his eyes should be was a sickly looking whiteness. Then the color of his face turned a dark blue.

"Mom!" Norman yelled and ran to the door.

Mom ran out, grabbed Kenny's shoulders, and shook him. Ken gave a sharp gasp, opened his mouth so that water ran out, and then he started to cough. We were relieved when Mom walked him into the house. But we had wakened Dad, and he appeared in his wrinkled slacks and his white undershirt.

He pointed at Norman and me. "You two, out back."

Our butts and the back of our legs got swipes from a tree branch. Norman took it, but I couldn't handle it. When we went in the house, Mom was crying, calling us wild horses. That bothered me more than the whipping. However, it wasn't the first time or the last time we caused her to shed tears. Later I realized something. Dad's whippings didn't bother me as much as they used to.

Norman turned ten. I thought he would always be the leader in our games, but something was happening to him. His change puzzled me. He didn't seem interested in the games we made up. He began to chase girls the last months of school.

On weekends we watched Grandpa's TV instead of going to Ashland. It was cheaper entertainment. *The Ed Sullivan Show* seemed all right except for him. He hunched his shoulders up, said "shew" instead of "show" and his eyes were too large. Guess I was getting picky for my entertainment choices.

Milton Berle had a TV show, but I didn't sleep much the first time I watched it. I stared in disbelief when he came on stage wearing a woman's dress. I wondered if people actually did things like that.

Most laughed at him, but I had a puzzled look on my face each time he dressed that way.

During the summer of 1950, Dad took us to the horse races often. We picked up tickets, and once we found one worth five dollars. Dad used it to buy Norman's first bicycle. Yes, life was beginning to look up.

Some days we could play for hours. When it was hot, we would take off our shirts. Our skin turned a healthy summer brown. Norman began to show muscles, but Mick, Ken, and I stayed bone thin.

As long as we stayed out of neighbors' yards, we could play anywhere in the village. We played near the grain elevator until farmers arrived with their corn crop. The stockyard on the south end became our fort away from home. Wann was our little kingdom and we became experts of making something out of nothing.

Wann could be an Indian village, an army fort, a make-believe gangster town. Wann could be a battlefield where our imaginations would run wild as to what we had heard on the radio and seen in picture shows. The sandy roads were our getaway trails.

We listened to new songs. The most popular were "Tennessee Waltz", "On Top of Old Smoky", and "Mockin' Bird Hill".

Once Grandpa installed that new invention, a television set, we began to learn more about them. Then we heard that Roy Everman, the man with the red chickens, had a TV set. *Must of got rich selling those brown eggs*, I thought.

Sept. 46

Mar. 3, 1948

May 48

June 48

July 48

Apr. 30, 1950

May 14, 1950

96

3rd Grade   May 1950

April 28, 1950

CHAPTER TEN

SUMMER, 1950

One summer night it was so hot; we stayed outside chasing lightning bugs until bedtime. We washed off at the outside pump and then to bed.

Before lights out Dad announced, "Everyone up early. Let you know why in the morning."

We pleading to know until he said, "Shut it up and go to sleep."

We woke when the sunshine streamed in the east window.

"Get ready. We're all going to the races today."

I couldn't remember the last time the family had driven to Lincoln. Maybe months ago for a Wells and Frost trip. Day after day we had survived, raced on the sandy roads, desired candy in the store, watched black locomotives blast past Wann, and now this trip.

Dad dressed in blue slacks, a white long-sleeve shirt over an undershirt, and his businessman's grey hat. My brothers and I wore faded jeans and scuffed-up brown shoes. What made us look country was our buttoned-up to the neck short-sleeve shirts.

"Look," I whispered to Norman, "Mom's wearing her Sunday dress." It was a white cotton design with large pink flowers.

We piled into Dad's car and then he drove across the Wann railroad tracks. Dad aimed his car toward Ashland on the gravel roads. I sat up and tried to learn the route. I counted the four iron-rusted bridges that we crossed.

After Mom had snapped her gum a few times, Dad told her to stop. She held Elaine tight and turned her head away from him. *Oh no*, I thought, *we can't have fights on our big day.*

The town of Ashland was a magical kingdom. We had been there at night with the lights and crowds and cars and picture shows. The town's streets were made of rust-red bricks. I thought no one here had to walk around water puddles as we did. And houses! Not shanties or low-roofed frame houses. These were real houses, some made of bricks.

Norman hit my arm and said, "Look."

There were three girls walking down a sidewalk. They were wearing shorts which showed off their brown legs. I never took notice of the bare legs of a Wann farm girl.

Norman whispered, "Look at the big butt. Looks like two hogs trying to fight their way out of a gunny sack."

He strained his neck to watch the girls then turned and grinned. It seemed that he was getting tired of our Wann games. Something else was on his mind, I could tell.

Wann had one store; Ashland had stores with cement sidewalks in front. Blocks and blocks of stores. A drug store. A feed store. One bank, one bus stop, and one movie theater. Two grocery stores, three beer joints, and one snooker hall.

Dad parked in front of the Town Tap and hustled in. When he came out, he said, "Got two free passes from Welch."

The whole trip so far was worth a month's learning out of school books. I tried to remember everything I saw. Dad crossed the Salt Creek Bridge and drove onto Highway 6. We were traveling on hard pavement, just like the large cement slab in front of our house. Not sand like the Wann roads or bricks like the Ashland streets.

As the car picked up speed, Dad pointed out and said, "Look at that freight train. Betcha a dollar I can beat it to Lincoln."

We saw the red caboose, but it was fleeing away. Dad sped up and we cheered him. After six miles, Dad pulled ahead of the caboose and passed boxcars and oil tankers. But the train's engine was still not is sight.

"Dammit, have to slow down for Greenwood."

The burg of Greenwood wasn't as large as Ashland. There was a reduced speed limit as the highway ran through it. The freight train blew its whistle and sped on. Dad lost ground. At the other side of Greenwood, he began to speed up.

"Come on, come on, move it!" Dad cried.

A slow moving farm truck cruised ahead of us.

"Watch out!"

Dad yelled as the truck slowed down to turn. We saw a car coming toward us in the other lane. Dad swerved the wheels to the right. He passed the truck on the outside, two tires off the pavement. My brothers and I slid to the right into a pile of arms and legs.

Mom said something. Dad told her to keep quiet.

Dad steered the car back on the highway. He was gaining on the train when Mickey shouted, "Look. There's the engine."

"Damn, guess the race is over. Have to slow down for Waverly."

Waverly was the size of Ashland, and it had a stop light. The train picked up speed. Dad stopped his car.

"Why'd you stop Dad?" Kenny asked.

"See that light? It's red. Means stop."

I asked, "How long do we wait?"

"Damn. You boys know nothing. When the light turns green we go."

So I learned about electric lights. The light flashed green; Dad stomped on the pedal, the tires squealed, and we sped through Waverly. It was hard to believe that Dad was having a good time with us.

He tore after the train while we held on to the back of the front seats. We watched him gain on the locomotive and its trailing black smoke. Maybe he was speeding, but we knew nothing about laws and state troopers.

"Look ahead, boys. We have to cross that overpass before the engine passes under it."

I saw the overpass. Highway 6 made a sharp curve to the right and into Lincoln. Cars and trucks went up and over, trains went underneath. Dad passed the engine and flew up and around the curve. Mom screamed, "Slow down!" Dad won the race, and then he laughed.

I felt drained. The Corn Flakes I ate bubbled up to my throat. With Dad we had competed and won. I felt a burning desire to contend, felt like a winner and not like a poor country boy.

I wondered what Mom thought. Did she like the racing and betting and the competition as much as we did? Did she wonder what would become of her four sons? When Dad won at the races, we ate more food and Mom bought us Sunday school clothes. When he lost, our house was quiet.

Dad drove into the outskirts of Lincoln. Wann was a village, Ashland was a town, but Lincoln was a magnificent city and it had us surrounded.

"First to see the capitol!" Dad cried out. "Boys, if ever one of you sees the capitol building before I do, I'll give you a quarter. See the gold dome?"

I strained to see where he pointed. The city of Lincoln seemed to go on and on. I couldn't determine the boundary of it. I saw trees, houses, and buildings taller than the Wann elevator. Finally, I saw the tallest building, and I caught a glimpse of gold color.

Mom said, "That's the state of Nebraska's capitol building. It's one of the ten most beautiful buildings in the United States."

"We're going downtown. Get something for lunch."

Dad was our guide. At last, he parked in front of a block of dilapidated brick buildings. He gave Mom a few dollars, told her to get a loaf of bread and minced ham. Then he turned around and looked at us.

"You boys sit still for a few minutes. I have business to attend. Keep the windows rolled down if you want."

We watched him walk down the block and enter a brick building. The sign above the door said—LUCKY'S PAWN SHOP—WE BUY, SELL, TRADE.

We watched the people walk by. Men with hats like Dad's. Everyone seemed to be moving in a hurry. I realized we had been sheltered by living in Wann. We never had a glimpse of what was going on in the big world.

Next to our car we noticed an old man behind the steering wheel of one of the oldest cars I had even seen. It looked like a box on wheels with four doors. The man's hands rested on the steering wheel, and his head drooped.

"Oh, oh."

Norman pointed to a tall girl and her mother who were bearing down on the old man. The girl was as plain as her clothes. She looked as if she had stayed home all her life. But the old lady! She was short, carried two packages, and hurried as fast as she could walk. She looked like a withered crab apple and walked like a bow-legged cowboy. Each step she took clopped down so hard we could hear it. Our eyes were on her as she swung open her door.

"Pa, where the hell you been Pa?"

The old man's head came up only to be hit by a shopping bag. The fierce old lady got in, the girl took her seat in the back, and the verbal abuse the man received was lost to us as he drove off.

We looked at each other wondering to laugh or not. Norman became restless after a few minutes.

"Watch this," he said.

He leaned over the front seat. Dad had left the key. The car was a stick shift so when Norman turned the key the engine coughed and sputtered. The car jumped backwards which caused us to bounce and giggle.

After another minute, Norman leaned forward to give us an extra bounce. Just as he turned the key, I saw Dad coming toward us. No time to give a warning.

"The hell's going on? Can't I leave you damn kids for one minute without you raising hell? Look at the car. Two feet out in the street. Dammit, I've got a good mind to blister your butts and take you home."

We sat there, eyes down, kept quiet. You don't tattle on your brothers. It was us against Dad. He said he was going to take us to the races, so he had better keep his word. He started the car and moved it back to the curb.

Mom arrived and said, "All I could find."

She handed each of us two crackers. She opened two sardine tins. She told us to put two sardines between our crackers.

"They need milk or water," she said.

"They can get a drink under the grandstand."

Dad backed up and drove to the racetrack. The parking lot looked bigger than the entire Wann village. We piled out and wanted to run and explore. Mom herded us into the cave-like opening under the grandstand. Kids got in free. Dad handed over his two free passes.

We were all eyes as we formed up behind Mom. Dad bought a racing program for 20 cents and then 25 cents for a Blue Sheet. I wondered how he always seemed to have money. I wished he had more, since then we gained candy and soda.

He said, "Boys, down that way is the bathroom. You know how to use a flush urinal, don't you?"

Grandma had a toilet in her house. It seemed like a magical toy. Just push down a lever and everything disappeared with a flushing sound.

"Let's go up in the grandstand. Show you where I sit. Then you can walk around. Don't get in anyone's road. You hear me? Keep the hell away from the betting windows and the cashiers. If you behave, I'll buy you a soda later."

We followed him out into the open-air grandstand. I figured the top seats were higher than the Wann elevator. Dad sat down to study the program.

Norman said to me, "Let's go to the bathroom."

We walked down the stairs and underneath the grandstand. My mind had settled down, so I became aware of smells. I liked the odor of cigarette and cigar smoke. The reek of horse manure drifted from the horse stables. Frying hamburger grease aroma floated over from a lunch counter outside the grandstand.

However, what they called a restroom stunk worse that our outhouse on a steamy day. It had one stool behind a swinging door. We stared at a yellow-stained tin fixture hanging high against the wall. A man had just finished using it. He turned to look at us as he zipped up his pants.

"You got to be a man to use this one," he said.

We waited until he left. We stood on tiptoes to do our business. Then we started exploring. Norman led the way as we walked into each booth. We had learned the concept of finders' keepers and thought nothing of pocketing anything we found.

As we walked past the grandstand opening, Norman pointed outwards and said, "Look at all those taxis."

Five or six yellow cars with signs on top were unloading gamblers. Cabs or taxis, it didn't make any difference to me. In one day, I was storing memories to last a year.

Norman grabbed my arm and pointed at a cab driver who was lounging on his cab's fender. "Look."

I glanced where he pointed. I stared at a man whose skin was black. I stood still, afraid to move. The man was studying a cigarette. He took a long drag on it. Slowly he let the smoke escape from his mouth. Then his face partially disappeared behind the cloud of smoke.

Norman pulled me aside, so we hurried back to the family. We were just in time because Dad said, "Let's go watch them saddle up in the paddock."

We followed Dad down the stairs and out onto the cement apron in front of the grandstand. It was a weekday, so the crowd was small. Dad walked to the edge of the grandstand and stopped alongside a wooden fence.

"Look at the thoroughbreds."

We crowded the fence on each side of him. There were eight stalls and a horse in each. The strong odor of horse manure mixed with cigarette smoke and human sweat.

Two or three men handled each horse. One man was checking a saddle that looked small enough for a kid. Three of the horses were nervous and sweaty, couldn't keep their feet still. Dad said they had jimmy legs. The others stood motionless. Then I saw something more fascinating than the black man.

The jockeys appeared and each went to his mount. Their uniforms looked sleek and shiny. They all wore white pants, but their jerseys were different colors. None of them looked taller than Norman. Yet they weren't young boys; each had a man's face. I thought they looked like freaks, yet everyone accepted them.

Each jockey carried a black whip. A pair of goggles sat on their bright colored caps. The men gave them instructions, and then gave the jocks a boost up on the horse. A bugle sounded. The jockeys paraded the horses onto the track. Never in my life had so many unusual and fascinating things happened on the same day.

"I'm going to bet now," Dad told us, "go back and sit with your mother."

For fun we ran up different stairs, clear to the top where no one sat. We were in the shade, and there was a whiff of a breeze blowing across our faces. We saw pigeon poop where it had fallen down from the rafters. We noticed Dad back with Mom, so we skipped down.

"Okay boys. I bet ten dollars on Mean Man to win. He's number four, so you better cheer for him."

The announcement, "Post time in two minutes" built excitement within me.

The jockeys moved the horses toward a long green machine that a tractor was pulling across the track. Kenny asked Dad what that was.

"It's the starting gate. Now sit down. They're about to run."

With a strong whiff of fresh cigar smoke sticking in my nose, I watched the horses as they moved into the gate. They stood still; an electrifying silence quieted the grandstand. All of a sudden a loud bell rang, gates flew open, out jumped the horses, the crowd yelled, and an announcer sang out "THEY'RE OFF!"

Dad jumped up so we did also. The horses flew past the grandstand in a group as I held my breath. The jockeys hunched forward; their butts up off the saddle. Clumps of dirt flew up behind the horses. A few jockeys reached back and swatted with their whips. In the background, I heard the announcer call out horse's names.

"Mean Man ahead by two lengths. They're rounding the far curve. They're entering the stretch."

I noticed Dad standing and yelling. He folded his program in half and whipped his hip with it. Maybe he had become the jockey in spirit.

I heard Mom yell as I caught the announcer's call.

"Down the stretch, it's Mean Man by two lengths, Mean Man by a length. Little Bud closing fast. At the wire, it's Little Bud by a nose."

I watched the two horses cross the finish line. Their jockeys stood up as the horses began to slow down. The rest of the field followed them.

"Dammit. Somebody jinxed me," Dad said. He tore his ticket and scattered it in the air. Mom sat still.

I felt overcome by an exhilarating feeling. I loved to run and race even though I always followed Norman. Yet another feeling entered. What an exciting way to make money. My heart was on fire because of that horse race.

I wanted to test my brain and bet money on my hunches. I longed to read the Daily Racing Form and the program. I couldn't wait till the next race. I wondered if I could watch horses exercising and pick the winner.

I glanced at Dad. Right then I saw him in a new light. He wasn't perfect. He made mistakes like anyone else. Suddenly everything seemed clear. When Dad had money he lost it. That's why our house has no indoor plumbing. That's why it's too small for a family of seven.

Dad said, "Norman and Warren, come with me."

We followed him until he stopped by a trash barrel. He picked out a Cracker Jacks box and gave it to Norman. At the next barrel, he found one for me. It looked like someone had spit tobacco juice on it.

"Okay boys, look around. See the tickets that people throw away? Walk around and pick them up. Full your boxes. I'll mark my program. We'll check your tickets when we get home. Sometime people throw away good ones."

I was pissed. I wanted to watch the horses and study the program to see if I could pick a winner. Instead, Norman and I raced each other when we saw a discarded ticket. We would stop and watch each race.

I spotted a tall man wearing overalls doing the same thing we were doing. Except he didn't bend over and pick up tickets. He had marked his program and would look down at a ticket and then check it. If a ticket was face down, he would slide one edge of his shoe under it and flip it over. We watched him for a while then ran ahead to get our share.

Norman got me over in a corner and said, "Look what I picked up."

He opened his hand to reveal a crumpled-up pack of Camel cigarettes, just like Grandpa smoked. Inside were three cigarettes, slightly bent.

"Whatcha going do with them, Norm?"

"Take 'em home. We'll smoke them tomorrow."

Just then Mom came up with our two younger brothers and Elaine. Norman hid his booty.

"Your dad won ten dollars. We're going to the lunch stand for supper."

We crossed the oiled road to the stand. Mom let us sit at the outside counter to watch the burgers fry. When the counterman tossed a slab of pink meat on the grill, I listened to the sizzle and watched it change from pink to brown. We ordered soda pop. By the time we finished Dad appeared.

The ride home was no fun. Dad lost all his winnings. There were no trains to race or landmarks to spot. I nodded off sometimes but kept my box of tickets clutched to my chest.

When I asked Dad if we could go to the races again, he said, "Hell no. You all jinxed me."

I was glad to see our building at last. Dad told us to go to bed; we'd check the tickets in the morning.

For breakfast we ate mushy oatmeal with sugar and a pat of butter since there was no milk. We cleared off the table, and then Norman and I did the dishes. He washed them in a container of hot water. I dried them. What did the two little farts do? Nothing, they just played with broken tinker toys. I couldn't wait till it was their turn to do the dishes.

Next, Dad made us spread our tickets out on the table. I loved the sorting by races. Then we read off the number on the ticket and Dad checked the first two races against his program. Then he let Norman and me finish. No winners, but we kept the tickets to play with in our made-up games. Dad told us to pick up tickets each time we went to the races.

"You might get lucky like your old man."

Mom told us, "Get ready to go to Grandpa's strawberry patch to pick."

When Dad walked to the store, Norman pocketed three matches from the match holder on the kitchen wall. He motioned me outside. We sat down in the weeds and rested against the back of the outhouse. Norman pulled out the Camels. I was nervous as hell but wanted to be included in his activities.

"Here's how you do it," he said.

He stuck a cigarette in his mouth then lit the match. He held the match to the end of his cigarette and sucked in air. It lit on fire. He opened his mouth to let the smoke out. I did the same but smoke caught in my throat. When I began to cough, Norman laughed.

We had puffed our cigarettes halfway down when we heard a shoe step on the weeds. We looked up at Dad.

He looked at us for a few seconds, "Hand over your smokes, boys. Now, you got any more?"

Norman handed him the last one. I kept my head down. Go ahead and whip, I thought, I just wanted to get it over with. I hoped Mom wouldn't find out because I felt that we had let her down.

Dad twisted the cigarettes into the ground to put them out.

"How about matches?"

Norman pulled one out of his pocket and gave it up.

Dad looked at us. "You boys stay right here. I'll be back in a minute."

"What do you think, Norm? Belt, yardstick, or a tree branch?"

He pulled up weeds and threw them away, then, "Dammit all to hell."

Dad was back without a punishment stick. He squatted down in front of us.

"Boys, I want you to try real tobacco. See what happens."

He pulled out a round container and twisted off its lid. We saw strands of brown leaf, and it smelled sweet. The word Redman was on the lid.

"Now look," he said, "pinch some between your fingers and thumb. Squeeze it together; put it in your mouth. Be careful, don't swallow any of it. Chew it into a ball. Move it to the side of your mouth. How's it taste?"

I was scared but knew I had to do what he said. I noticed Dad didn't chew any. The tobacco had a sweet taste.

"Now, I want you to get your hoes and work on these tomatoes. Cut the weeds and then pull dirt up around the roots. After thirty minutes stop to pick strawberries. Remember, keep that wad in your mouth. Spit the juice out any time you want. But don't swallow any. Got that?"

We chewed and spat. Looked at each other and laughed. We got our hoes and went to work on the garden.

"What's up, Norm? Aren't we going to get whipped?"

"Don't know, maybe Dad's helping us grow up."

What the hell, I thought. Chew and spit. Actually, I thought I was getting some nourishment from the wad. We were done after twenty minutes, but I began to feel kinda funny. The summer sun beat down on the back of my head. I began to sweat and feel sick. I reached down to pull a weed, and when I rose up, wow, I felt dizzy in the head. Sick of the tobacco, I spit mine out.

"Norm, I'm sick as hell. Think I'm going to puke."

He grabbed my hoe and told me to sit down on the shed's step.

"Put your head down between your knees. See if that helps."

I saw Norman spit out his wad. Hung my head down but that didn't help the dizzy feeling. *My head's out of control*, I thought. Just then Mom came looking for us.

"Let's go boys, time to work. Remember, your Grandpa pays a dime for every carton you fill."

I stood up too fast. Circles spun around my head, and my stomach came up to my throat. I bent over with my hands on my knees. Then the oatmeal came out in a hurry. It looked like traces of brown and green. Mom rushed over and held my head as I heaved twice more.

"What's wrong? Got the stomach flu?"

"I'm weak and dizzy, Mom. Just need to lie down."

Norman looked green in his face, but he went with Mom. I stumbled into the house. Dad was sitting at the table, reading the racing form. Elaine was asleep in the crib. I lay down on the couch and turned my head to the wall.

"Guess you'll stay away from tobacco for a while, huh?"

I felt he didn't deserve an answer.

Dad went to the races that afternoon and came home late. He said, "Got some bad news, but good music. Lost money today, but I brought a new record. My luck ain't worth shucks, but tomorrow I'll hit a lick."

Dad placed his record on the machine and turned it on. "Set 'em up, Joe" was the name.

"All my neon neighbors they like what I play, so set 'um Joe and play 'Walkin' the floor, I said set'em up Joe and play walkin' the floor."

He played it four or five times and hummed along with it. I felt better by night, but falling asleep was hard. That damn song kept running through my head. "Set 'em up Joe and play walkin' the floor." The harder I tried to put it out of my mind, the more it kept playing "Set 'em Joe and play walkin' the floor".

The next time Dad took us to the races he "hit a lick." He joked all the way back to Ashland.

Norman asked, "Can we get another hamburger at the Silver Café?"

"Nope," Dad said, "this time we'll go to a fancier place. The Calumet Café out on Highway 6. And you boys can taste French fries."

On the ride back to Wann I thought that our luck ran good today with no jinx.

CHAPTER ELEVEN

In the summer our screen door had rips in it, so Dad hung strips of flypaper from the main room's ceiling. I liked to examine the flies on the strip to see if any were struggling to unstick themselves. When the flypaper became black with dead flies, Dad tore it down and threw it into the garbage ditch across the road.

One of our favorite activities in the fall was to catch yellow leaves that drifted down from the cottonwood trees near our house. If there were the slightest breeze, we didn't have much of a chance.

"Catch it, Warren, get it!" Norman would yell to me.

If my older brother thought I could do something, I tried hard not to let him down. I would hustle this way and that way with a bushel basket, trying to catch the floating leaf. Mick and Ken tried to catch leaves in their baskets. Norman selected the harder route. He carried a galvanized pail; it had a smaller opening.

I thought Norman would always be the leader in our games, but something was happening to him. His change puzzled me. He didn't seem interested in the games we made up. He began to chase girls the last months of school.

The day we were catching leaves was a beautiful fall afternoon: Dad was gone; Mom was listening to a University of Nebraska football game. The dogs were sprawled in the shade. Occasionally, a freight train led by a black locomotive would chug by. Whenever we heard an airplane we would stare at the sky. Anything unusual grabbed our attention.

Dad was home on Sunday. We never knew what would happen when he was around. He would laugh at pranks between his brothers and sisters--like a bar of ten cent soap as a Christmas present. He could see omens. An open umbrella in the house would bring bad luck. If his lucky pen were missing, he would blame that on his losing bets.

This Sunday we washed up for Sunday school and the church service at the Wann Christian Church. If it were hot, my brothers and I would fight over who got the cardboard fan in our pew. If Dad weren't watching, we would wave the fan in our closest brother's face, just to piss him off.

After we walked home, we had one of our better meals—Mom's crispy fried chicken with mashed potatoes and gravy. Afterwards,

Dad announced, "Boys, get your sacks. We're going for a drive. Never know what we might find."

I raced Norman back to the shed. He threw out two Idaho Potato gunnysacks and two Miller Seed Corn sacks. We jumped in the back seat of Dad's Chevy. Mom and Elaine sat in front. A few miles west of Wann, Dad began to cruise along the gravel road. He fancied himself as a great teacher, today's lesson being "finders' keepers."

"Apple tree, boys. Norman and Warren, go over the fence."

All four of us piled out carrying our sacks. Mick and Ken picked up apples in the ditch. Norman held down the barbwire fence for me to cross over. Dad got out and supervised, but he left the car running. Mom stayed in the car, our lookout. This excitement caused a twist in my gut. If our bounty were plentiful, we gained approval from Dad. But there was always the danger of a farmer driving down the road catching us trespassing.

Quickly, we picked up bruised apples and those hanging low on the tree. Most were wormy. Then we jumped over the fence like scared rabbits and piled back into the car. Sometimes Dad would start moving slowly, and we would jump in on the run. We loved it.

If the apples were half rotten, Mom would cut out the best parts and stew applesauce. Better yet, sometimes she would make apple butter, a light brown spread for a slice of bread. Then we were living high on the hog.

At times a fruit tree would be further out in a pasture field. All of us slid under the fence and made a quick grab, then ran for the car. Sometimes we would spy a black walnut tree. The walnuts would be scattered along the road and in the ditch. These became captive also.

"Mom, now you can make walnut fudge."

On our journey back to Wann, Dad slowed down as he drove past a two-story farmhouse located down a dirt lane. Back of the house was a massive red barn surrounded by pens and chicken sheds. Painted in white letters across the front of the barn was H. P. VonBusch, 1899.

We saw calves and pigs in separate pens. Chickens of various colors were scratching in the yard; two brown horses were eating hay out of a bunk. We were hushed as we stared at the prosperity of the farm family. *Something we're never going to experience*, I thought.

Dad stopped a quarter mile from the farm lane. He pointed to a flock of white geese paddling down the road ditch which was half full of irrigation water.

"Norman, come with me," Dad said. To the rest of us, "Keep an eye on that farmhouse."

I watched Norman jog down the road to get behind the geese. Dad stayed near until the geese arrived, and then he hustled down into the ditch. The geese scattered in all directions while honking in panic, like a misguided fire drill.

"Grab one!" Dad yelled at Norman.

Both of them were knee deep in the water. I watched Norman grab a squawking goose by its neck. He struggled out of the ditch and ran to the car. Dad had one by its yellow feet.

I thought, *this isn't finder's keepers, this is stealing.* When Norman jumped in the back seat, the goose fought for its life, flapping its wings and scattering loose gobs of manure. We jumped away from it. Then Dad pushed his towards me, and told me to keep it down. White feathers began to drift inside the car.

Dad spun the tires and made his getaway. Two miles later he stopped and told us to bring the geese behind the car. He broke their necks by whirling them around. Dad used two sacks to clean up the back seat. We drove to the bank building. Everyone sat in silence.

"Boys, help me skin these birds."

He told Mom to heat a pail of water and bring it back. When the birds were picked clean, he told me to dig a small hole in the pigpen. Mick and Ken picked up the feathers and buried them.

"We can't leave any evidence." Dad told us. "We'll roast the geese tomorrow."

That night I experienced a restless sleep due to the geese activity. I felt that Norman enjoyed the stealing action too much. He seemed prideful in helping to bring home food for the family, regardless of an ill-gotten gain.

Early the next day Grandma stepped in for a visit, and she appeared to be crying.

"Wendell joined the Army. Hope they don't send him to the war."

I thought about how we hadn't seen him for a while. Grandma said that he had been bumming around the state doing odd jobs. Somewhere in western Nebraska, Wendell walked into a recruiting station and signed up. He called home to say he was on his way to Ft. Riley in Kansas.

The message sent us boys outside to sit in the shed. I thought about how I missed Wendell. Then I looked at my little brothers and decided to treat them better than I had been doing. If one of them were gone, I would miss him also.

The world paid little attention to Wann, and we repaid in kind. A place called Korea didn't register with us. Wann was our universe except for the occasional trips to Ashland or Lincoln. Our everyday survival was more important than current events.

Would there be food for breakfast and of what nature? Where would the groceries for dinner and supper come from? If Dad was away on a gambling trip and didn't send money, how was Mom supposed to care for us?

Once Dad brought home raccoon meat. Mom fried it. We ate it. *A terrible scene all the way around*, I thought. The meat was too tough and tasted like fried heart but not near as good. The next day I asked Mom about the red splotches on my arms.

"You got the hives, probably from that damn coon meat."

Grandpa Sam stopped in to look at them.

"Be careful, if they get in his throat, it'll swell up. Then he won't be able to breathe. He'll be done for. Maybe if he sucks on horehounds them hives will wilt."

There was no doctor in Wann, but that didn't matter. Doctors want paid, and Dad's name was on the list. So I had to rest. Rest, that was the Wann cure for all sickness.

I stared at Grandpa as he made his statement. He gurgled down a half can of Pabst Blue Ribbon beer. I knew he favored Norman; he hardly ever talked to me. I watched him take a drag on his Camel cigarette, and wished Mom had some horehounds. They were like candy to me.

I coughed when his smoke drifted over me. I thought, *bullshit, I ain't gonna die.* Besides, I'd had chicken pox, mumps, measles, and severe constipation. I'm tougher than he thinks. I turned my head away.

Year after year, our Thanksgiving and Christmas celebrations never varied. Early on Thanksgiving morning we walked to Grandma's. We were the oldest grandkids. Uncle Larry and Aunt

Joann were a few years older, so they mixed between adults and us.

The house was crowded, cigarette smoke hung in the air, and Grandma and her helpers cooked in the small kitchen. The roast turkey aroma made me stop and take in deep breaths. I wanted to taste that smell. We walked from room to room, talking and listening.

"Kids to the table," was the first command.

The living room had one long table. Mom knew what I would eat and wouldn't. I would get a half bowl of potato soup since I couldn't eat much of it.

Next would be a plate. We began with as many sliced, homegrown tomatoes as we wanted. At the end of the tomato season, Grandpa had his family set aside half-ripened tomatoes. They wrapped each one in a sheet of paper and stored them in a cool place. In November and December, his family ate fresh tomatoes.

Our mothers filled our plates. Mom made sure I got white turkey meat with mashed potatoes and gravy, and a vegetable, beans or corn. Finally, the biggest treat of the year, better than any store candy. Red jello placed in a large, stemmed glass. On top of the jello was fresh whipped cream. Black walnut pieces were sprinkled on top of the whipped cream. The queen of England didn't eat this good.

Next, the adults cleared the table. They sat down and enjoyed the same meal as ours. Grandma's face stayed flushed from the kitchen heat. The kids moved to the kitchen and picked through large tins of nuts and hard candy.

When the adults finished most of them sat down to a game of poker. More cigarettes lit up; whiskey and beer filled their glasses. After dark the relatives would fill their cars and we would walk home. I had dreams that night of a large, happy family with plenty of food and treats.

A couple of crucial events added to the Christmas holiday. On Christmas Eve we would hike to the grandparents to meet the same relatives. The meal was oyster soup. I mixed crackers with the soup and got it down. I left the slippery oysters in the bottom of the bowl, and then snuck the bowl into the kitchen.

After supper the tension became unbearable. Dad or an uncle would sneak outside and ring a cow bell. All the kids would dance and shout, "It's Santa."

We would run to the windows and look and then to the kitchen to see if he had walked in. The youngest ones would cling to their mothers, scared of the commotion.

After what seemed liked an eternity, Santa marched in the kitchen door with a bag over his shoulder. Our mothers organized us into corners so that we kept our own presents. Sam and Maude always gave us one gift. Sometimes we received a gift or two from the aunts and uncles. For years the adults planned this evening without fail and without change.

"Look," Norman once whispered, "it's Grandpa in that Santa suit."

One time my present was a paper book that had more pictures than words. I asked Uncle Larry for help.

"This is a Hopalong Cassidy funny book," he said, "but nowadays people call them comic books."

All of us looked through the comic book, but it didn't last long. Soon pages were dirty and torn, so I threw it away.

The Christmas Eve events stayed the same as we aged. At the end of the evening, we would grab our presents and walk home. It would be hard going to sleep, since we knew that in the morning we could open our gift from Santa in our own home.

On Christmas morning we wanted to play with our new toys. Still, before dinner once again the walk took place. The procedure was similar to Thanksgiving. Kids ate first--tomatoes, turkey and mashed potatoes. Then the heavenly dessert of jello, whipped cream and black walnuts. The adults ate, smoked, drank and played poker for money. We walked home early so we had time to play with our new toys.

Christmas day held an extra treat for us—home-made candy. Grandpa made his out of rich cream, sugar, and bitter chocolate. He mixed cream and sugar in a cake tin, and then he spread a thin layer of chocolate over it. After it cooled he cut it into squares. I loved it, but it was too rich. Didn't make any difference, no one could take more than two pieces.

Grandma's outstanding candy was a chopped date and nut mixture that looked like a roll of sausage. This was my favorite. I would eat more than one piece if I had the opportunity. Our aunts and uncles told us that the candies were made early and then hidden, but they always discovered the hiding places. Grandma and Grandpa then had to remake the treats.

Once Miss Barta announced that on the day before Christmas vacation, we would play games. One was bob for apples. When school let out I ran home.

"Mom, we're going to bob for apples tomorrow. Can I use the water pail and practice?"

"We only got one apple in the house, but go ahead."

After supper, I filled the pail with water and sat it on the kitchen floor. I dropped the apple in, and then tried to get my teeth into it. The brothers gathered around, argued about whose turn it was, pushed and shoved. We slopped water on the floor.

Dad came home and gave us hell for making a mess. Since it was my idea, I had to clean up and fetch fresh water. I had no better luck the next day. Jack Veskerna managed to bring one apple up, so he was better than me. I felt the shame as I walked home, but Grandma's Christmas was just around the corner.

During two Christmas seasons, Mom added a little spoiler. She called Norman and me to the table.

"Look at this Christmas card catalog. Take it to every house in Wann. Show it to people and ask if they want to buy a box or two. You earn twenty cents for every box you sell."

"Do we have to? Nobody has any money in Wann."

It seemed too much like begging to me. I wanted no part of it.

"Norman, you carry the catalog. Both of you take turns asking."

At each house, I prayed no one would answer the door. I was surprised. Most ordered one box and Grandma ordered two. Still, it felt like begging to me so I hated it. After two years, Mom forgot about the cards which made me happy and gave me time to explore the Sears Christmas catalog.

That winter, no matter how cold it was, we grew bored of staying inside. So when Larry and Joann showed up at our door with two wooden sleds, Norman and I bundled up. We walked over to the Wann elevator. We lay down on the sled and tried to steer it with the wooden handles. Down a slope we soared. If we reached the road there was a patch of ice which sailed our sled along.

One time Dad walked over with a diaper tied under his chin. His grey hat sat on top. He was too large for the sled, so he never made it to the bottom. And, he never got pissed when we laughed at his falling. Mom's hot lemonade that night made me think that the world was fair. We would survive. The Russian commies wouldn't dare attack.

CHAPTER TWELVE

1951

Without even a Ladies Aid warning, the unexpected happened. Almost dusk, I sat reading my Christmas book from Grandma--Tarzan and the City of Gold. A car horn honked, and someone yelled. The phone rang, and Dad grabbed the receiver.

My head turned from Dad's conversation to Aunt Arlene rushing in our house.

"Did you hear the news?"

Dad on the phone. "Hey, you expect me to believe that?"

"Here, right here in Wann." Arlene again.

"Yeah, I was born at night, but not last night."

"Going to be at the church."

"Okay, okay, hold your horses. Arlene's here." Dad hung up.

Arlene said, "Boys, she's coming to Wann, to the Fellowship Hall. Aunt Jemima's coming. And she's cooking free pancakes."

I sat there, stunned. The Tarzan book slid from my hands. Aunt Jemima? That dark lady pictured on a pancake mix box? You mean she's a real person? And coming to Wann? And did I hear correctly, pancakes? And the one word so special to us--free?

Dad said, "Otis just called. Three weeks from now. Free pancakes and sausage. All you can eat."

Well, if that didn't put the frosting on the cake. I couldn't think of any sentence better than this—all you can eat pancakes, free. No, this couldn't happen. The weather would turn nasty, there would be a traffic delay, Aunt Jemima would find out Wann was not a town. I wanted to believe, but I steeled myself for disappointment.

The fellowship hall connected to the church's chapel. The hall had a small stage at one end where our school presented Christmas programs. Wann mixers took place in the hall.

A mixer was a local talent show of singing, accordion playing, poem reciting, and short skits. A Wann original of made-up entertainment. Each Mixer played to a full house. Eventually, the TV ended the mixers.

Two rows of long benches faced the stage. The kitchen was off to one side. That's where Aunt Jemima would prepare her free pancakes.

However, one thing bothered me. Due to our limited supply of foodstuff, we were taught to share and share alike. No one got more than anyone else. If you swiped extra walnut fudge, one of your brothers would report. Therefore, to go through the serving line more than once seemed to me as something not quite right. Greedy I was, yes, but I didn't want all of Wann to witness my action.

The day finally arrived with grey clouds which turned ugly black. The morning hours seemed to last all day. Terrible clouds rolled around and centered on Wann. They teased us with distant thunder and then finally boomed over our heads. I knew it. The gravel road from Ashland to Wann would flood. Aunt Jemima's pancake parade would go to Wahoo instead. The rain hammered down for ten minutes. Then the weather changed its mind and whisked the clouds away.

By suppertime we were ready with clean jeans and T-shirts. We sat on our cement slab waiting for farmers to drive up. *We're only one block from paradise*, I thought.

Dad warned, "Don't act like a pack of hungry dogs in a butcher shop."

Five cars pulled up to the church. Mom and Dad stepped out dressed up. Dad with his hat, white shirt and slacks. Mom in her best cotton print dress. We practically jogged that one block.

On the north side of the hall, there were two panel trucks full of Aunt Jemima's supplies. Then I saw her when she walked into the hall. She wore a large flowery dress, but what I noticed most was her face. Not only was she the deliverer of free and all you can eat, I thought she had the face of an angel.

Norman and I looked to see if a line had formed. Wholesome coffee aromas circled the air. I could hear sausage sizzling. Womenfolk bustled with the plates, cups, napkins and forks. Outside the traditional groups formed.

The farmers talked crops and smoked. Older singles flirted while sitting on the fenders of cars. Norman and his buddies organized a chase-the-girls game down the back alley. Suddenly, Norman pulled a cute farm girl toward me and said, "It's your turn."

What the heck did he mean? Turn for what? He placed her arm in my hands. I looked at her as she tucked her blouse into her skirt with her other hand. She looked at me. I wondered if I walked her down the alley, then what.

She said, "Nelda says you can't kiss worth a hoot or a holler."

She yanked her arm away and ran back to Norman's gang.

Relieved, I walked near the door. I didn't need to be first in line, but I wanted to be close. My stomach growled when I overheard words like flapjacks, hotcakes, and griddle cakes.

"Head 'em up," was called from inside. The door jammed with people. I paired up with a classmate, Jack Veskerna, and then we were in the hall. Jack and his twin sister, Judy, lived on a farm two miles north of Wann.

Our line reached the counter. We grabbed forks, napkins, and a plate with two pancakes and two links of sausage. I poured on syrup and hustled to a bench.

With our plates balanced on our laps, they became empty in no time. My stomach hardly felt the first serving. I glanced at the line and noticed people with empty plates, already on their second visit.

"Let's go, Jack."

We reached the end of the line and placed our dirty plates in a large tub. I watched Mom wash and dry and then restack the clean plates. Grandma was in the serving line, and when she saw me, she placed five sausage links on my plate.

"Take these," she said, "put some meat on your bones."

I gave her my gap-tooth smile, and then headed for another bench. My stomach protruded a little after that plate. Jack said he was finished, so I found Norman, and we entered the line once again. Three trips did it for me. Just as I took my last bite there was a stir in the hall.

"Free ice cream cones!"

Boy howdy, can you beat that? Someone carried in two large cartoons of strawberry and chocolate from the Ashland creamery. I found out I wasn't as full as I thought. When done, I looked around at the people.

I thought, *this is what life is all about*. Everyone seemed cheerful about the night. It was an enthusiastic group gathering of neighbors, relatives, and Wann people. What more out of life would anyone want? Let the uppity people in Ashland stick their noses up at us in the lower class. Nothing they could undertake would exceed this night. I think Dad disliked some Ashland people because their bank wouldn't lend him money without any backing.

Suddenly, the lights felt hot. My skin broke out into a clammy sweat. My stomach began to feel the way a manure spreader looked out in a field, throwing its load in all directions. I tore out of the hall and made it halfway home. Then I stopped and vomited in the ditch.

When we went to Sunday school the next time, we read Psalms. Mine was, "So they ate the food of angels, and God gave them all they wanted." My mind forgot the lesson while I thought of free pancakes, sausages, and ice cream. We were the tribe who ate the food of angels.

By this time, all of us brothers attended the Wann Elementary. Norman had the job of sweeping the hall and the big room—grades five through eight—every night after school for twenty-five cents per day. Sometimes I helped by spreading the red sawdust that put a shine on the wooden floors when swept up.

It seemed as if every picture show we attended was a western. We watched John Wayne and Jimmy Stewart, but our favorite movie was "The Gunfighter" starring Gregory Peck. Dad told us, "You boys can't watch Gene Autry in the movies anymore. Just read he's going to make TV shows."

That year Dad bought each of us a calf. We could name it, water it, and take care of it. I wondered what happened to the money when the grown calf disappeared. If Dad thought we were a little pissy about the situation, he would throw us a quarter and tell us to go over to the store. All I knew was that the calf was gone, and I'd bet that soon the money would be gone also. Usually, we would never see a red cent.

One spring Saturday morning, Dad told Norman and me to go take care of our calves.

"Boys, I'm short on cash. Can't buy feed. Get them out of the barn, bring them over to the ditch and stake them out."

There was a gusty wind blowing from the northeast, occasional sheets of rain would sweep across Wann. Our jackets were thin, our gloves had holes in them, but we did have overshoes. They were black with seven buckles down the front. Norman had a cap with earmuffs. I pulled on a stocking hat.

We leaned into the wet wind the two blocks to Grandpa's barn. I felt bitter. Sure, Dad had paid for the calves. But we did all the work for no pay. If they got loose, it was our fault.

When we reached the barn, we shook the water off and warmed

up. The barn produced a nasty manure smell, so we had to be careful where we stepped.

After we had hooked our lead ropes to their halters, I asked Norman, "You sure we need to take them out in this weather?"

"Better do what we're told."

Just then the wind struck the barn with a dangerous gust. The wind howled and the barn began to groan. I thought there were scary voices wailing outside. Then the creaking sound became louder, the calves tried to pull away from us, and one side of the barn began to fall outwards.

"Watch out!" Norman yelled as my calf bolted into me and knocked me down.

I looked up as the roof slowly dropped toward me. By the time I started to pick myself up, one part of the rafters had reached my shoulder and pushed me down. I felt a sharp pain and then the heavy pressure of the beam pinned me.

"Crawl out, Warren, get out!" Norman cried.

I glanced up and saw him straining with both hands, trying to keep the roof from coming down any further. The boards had me trapped, I couldn't crawl forward. The calves moved to a safe area.

"Don't think I can move."

"Hold on." Norman said.

He grabbed two ten-gallon feed pails and shoved them under the rafters. I heard Norman screaming for help. Finally Norman ran back from the side that was still standing. Grandpa was with him. They tried to raise the rafters off me.

"What the hell's going on?" I heard Dad and watched him climb through the manger. Him and Grandpa forced timber under a fallen rafter which raised it up. Then Norman gabbed under my shoulders and pulled me out.

I felt shaky, but aware of different activities during the next hour. I was in the back of Dad's car, and Mom was crying. The bouncing of the car didn't help my bruises.

I heard Dr. Williams in Ashland say, "He needs stitches in a hospital."

Dad said, "I can't afford that."

"The Children's Hospital in Omaha will take him."

I drifted in and out of sleep. In the hospital a doctor cleaned and stitched my back, an x-ray showed just a bruised shoulder, one night in the hospital was required.

At noon the next day Norman walked into my room with a big grin on his face.

"Hey, you ought to see all the babes around here."

"Yep, bet you like them all. But I want to go home."

He looked up as a student nurse walked in. He was almost a teenager and hot on the trail of any female.

He gave her a grin as he proclaimed, "I saved my brother's life."

She smiled at him, and then became competent as she took my temperature and blood pressure.

"How old do you have to be to be a nurse?" Norman asked her.

"Oh, about twenty or twenty-one."

As she walked out, Norman looked at her legs. Then he leaned toward me and whispered, "I think she likes me."

I remembered what Grandpa had told Dad a week ago. "That Norm, he's feeling his wild oats fer sure."

Norman went to the door and looked down the hall. He ducked back in and said, "Candy stripers are coming."

I struggled out of bed to go to the bathroom. That damn gown, it never stayed closed in the back. I watched Norman walk over to the mirror to smooth his hair. He raised his arm to smell under his armpit. What a goof ball he was becoming.

When I came out, I grabbed the back of the gown because I saw two teenage girls. Norman was in his prime. I hustled under the bed sheet so they couldn't see my jockey shorts. They pushed a goodies cart to give away drinks and cookies. They said something to Norman that they were volunteers and hoped to become nurses. I thought the one who came over to me was cute.

"Would you like a drink?" She smiled at me.

Suddenly I felt that the word sweet and this girl were connected. My brain felt muddled, but I did manage to nod my head. Not only did the word sweet enter my mind, but also young, soft-skinned, and pretty hair and I couldn't help but focus on her cute eyes and soft lips, and where the hell did all that come from, I wondered.

"Here you go." Again, she smiled.

I wondered what to say to her, but nothing came to mind. Norman talked enough for both of us, and walked them to the door leaving me with a strange feeling. Maybe he had been feeling this way for the last year. The dreamlike atmosphere ended abruptly when Dad charged through the door and threw a bag of my clothes on the bed.

"Hurry up and get dressed. Got to get you home and back before the races start."

Yep, that was our life. All our actions and use of time depended on those damn horse races.

Anyway, Norman was leaving me behind with the homemade games and leaf catching and chase 'em races and chores. I felt terrible; I didn't want to experience change.

I remembered Norman once told me that he wanted a girlfriend who wore pink brassiere and panties. We were hoeing in Grandpa's tomato patch. Grandpa overheard him and said, "Remember this boys—keep your ding-a-ling in your pants. That's where it belongs."

It felt good to get home. The next day Dad felt necessary to put me in my place.

"When you're done with breakfast gather all the waste paper. It's your turn to take it out back and burn it."

When I finished my bowl of Cheerios a light rain had begun. Mom and the boys were playing a game of hide the thimble. I loved playing games, so I jumped right in.

A half hour later we stood at the screen door to watch the rain pour down. Dad walked over and looked out. "You get those papers burned?"

Oh hell. As I stood out in the rain trying to light a match, I felt like quitting. I never did anything right. However, I didn't get a spanking, just a cussing out.

Two months later, Dad invented another one of his rabbit pens. This one is a real money maker he told us. He explained that, at most race tracks, anyone could buy a Daily Racing Form and a program. The program listed the entries, odds, owners, trainers, and the names of the horse's parents. The form has the past performances of most horses that had been racing.

He said you could also buy a Blue Sheet. The Blue Sheet was a handicapper's picks for each race.

"I can do better that the Blue Sheet. I'm going to put my picks on a sheet, the Red Sheet. Get a bunch printed in Lincoln every morning. Sell them at the track at the country fairgrounds in Hastings."

"Can you make a lot of money?"

"If I get on a roll, everyone will want my picks. The Red Sheet will sell like hot cakes. Now here's what I want you boys to do."

He showed us a stack of thirty racing forms on the table. We gathered around, eager to help him make money.

"Mickey and Kenny, cut out each horse's past performance section. Norman and Warren, sort them by horse's name in alphabetical order. Then, when a horse is entered, I'll have a history of all its past races. This is a free lesson in bookkeeping."

We jumped to our jobs. Dad told us if he made good, we would make spending money. At the beginning, the mission went well. Dad organized places to arrange our sorts. Shortly, however, he decided that Mickey and Kenny couldn't cut out precise on-the-line rectangles.

"Doesn't that damn school teach you how to cut out?"

"Warren, get the scissors. See if you can do it."

The two little farts had to wash and dry the dishes. I was happy.

Soon, "Norman, if you're going to work that slow go do something else."

I liked the job. Soon I was the only one working. I would classify, separate, match and arrange. I continued this work until I got tired. But I never got bored. Norman would rather work with Grandpa.

Dad did a lot of studying and was ready for opening day. The Hastings race track allowed him to set up a small booth to sell his tout sheet, that's what he called it. We met him at the door the first night.

"Made just a little. My sheet had four winners out of eight. Tomorrow the word will get around. Going to sell more for sure."

The next morning he couldn't find his lucky pen. He even got pissed at me since the performance sheets he wanted weren't in order. When he came home that night he scratched the front bumper on a tricycle.

"One of you git out there and move that damn trike or I'll throw it away. I'm quitting the damn horses."

Mom dared to ask, "How did your sheet do?"

"Only had one winner. The money I made I lost on the eighth race. I'm done with 'em. Anyway, the word is they're shutting down the track. No crowds, small bets. Go to bed, all of you."

He was gone most of the next day. After supper we played outside until we heard Dad honk the horn. We scrambled out of his way. At first, I couldn't figure out what was wrong with his car. The trunk lid was up, and the back seat was sticking out of it. Behind Dad we saw a head. Norman ran to open the car door. Dad jumped out and yelled, "No!" It was too late.

A calf the color of Bambi uncorked her legs and stumbled out of the back seat. Dad ran around the back of the car cussing. "Grab it, grab it!" That energized all of us. Norman tried to tackle her back legs. I moved in front of the calf but she was too hefty. She head butted me, knocked me on my keister. Then the chase was on.

Bambi kicked up her hind legs and trotted behind the house. We gave chase with Dad's yells urging us on. Bambi ran into Mom's make-shift clothes line and caught her head on one of Dad's white shirts. She shook her head, and then loped into the school yard and scattered the red hens.

Norman sprinted in front of her and tried to grab her head. Meanwhile, Mom had called Grandpa's and Uncle Larry raced down the road in Grandpa's truck. He slammed to a stop and jumped out with a rope and halter.

Just before the calf tore into the Lehr's flower bed, Norman got a head lock on her. He dug in his heels as I helped him hold on. Larry placed the halter on her, took off Dad's shirt, and led her back up the road. Most of the clan had gathered at our house, so the telling and the retelling of the chase brought lots of laughs.

The result was Dad said the calf was Mom's and he thought it was a Jersey breed. Mom named it Bambi. Dad assigned Norman and I to fetch water and rags to wipe out the back of his car, just to remind us who was boss.

During the hot days of summer, horseflies attacked our house. They were twice as large as a normal fly, and their loud buzz could keep a drunk from sleeping. Since our screen door had rips, the flies invaded. When they irritated Dad, he told us to get out of the house since he was going to borrow Grandpa's sprayer.

When he returned, the sprayer looked like an interesting toy, so we trooped into the house after him. It was a red cylinder with a pump handle at one end and a small container for the spray at the other.

"Told you boys to get out. Now do it. Or maybe you want to get sick."

He pointed the sprayer at us and pumped it a couple of times. A misty cloud settled over us. We ran outside coughing. We waited for lunch until the stink of the spray faded.

The next day the flies returned. Dad borrowed fly swatters from Grandma. They featured a wire handle and mesh wire for the killing end.

"Give you boys a penny for each dead fly you bring me."

We had a hell of a time until Dad chased us outside again. Mickey knocked over a lamp, but it didn't break. The flies were easy to smack, so that's how we took care of them the rest of the year. We wondered if Dad remembered our payment and figured probably not.

CHAPTER THIRTEEN

1951

I turned ten the summer of '51. Major events were coming, but I didn't see them. Probably a good thing, I would have brooded too much. When Dad was gone, I quit worrying since Norman was eleven and both of us had BB guns for nightly protection.

In early June, after a breakfast of Wheaties and milk, Mom hiked us over to Grandpa's strawberry patch every other morning. We filled strawberry cartons, tried not to step on vines, and jumped if a garter snake scooted across our hand.

Uncle Larry drove Grandpa's panel truck to the patch to load up our pickings. He gave Mom the money, ten cents for each carton we filled. Mom allowed us to spend a dime at the store. Then the debate was on—race now for a soda and candy bar, or wait until after dinner and buy a fudgsicle and penny candy.

By July fourth, I had become too big for my britches. Acting too smart, playing the big-shot role, I tempted fate by playing with matches. In a Podunk where nothing ever occurred, the unbelievable happened.

The day was steamy hot with very little breeze, which was fortunate for me. After lunch relatives arrived. The adults played cards and drank beer.

The Washburn brothers and four cousins walked over to a shade tree by the store. We were out of firecrackers, but I had a few matches in my pocket. For excitement purposes, I lit the dry grass under the tree and encouraged all to stomp it out.

Twice I ran to our building for more ammunition. Twice Dad growled at me, "Behave with those matches. Stay out of trouble."

I was in too much of a hurry to take his warning to heart. When I returned to the group, I added a new twist.

"After I light the grass, wait to put it out until I say 'go.'"

I had four matches. Each time I waited a little longer to turn the guys loose. The fourth time I waited too long. We couldn't stop the grass fire. A light breeze spread the red flames northeast into a small wheat stubble field. Sitting at the corner of that block was the white-boarded Wann Christian church.

I ran. I screamed. The folks came running. Two cars stopped. The flames gathered strength and rose higher than the roof of the church. I found myself at our pump, but buckets of water couldn't stop the horror I had created.

Crying, screaming, and pumping, I had never been so scared. I watched red and black flames surge up and around like a funnel cloud. *This is what hell looks like*, I thought.

I heard the siren of the Ashland fire truck. Three miles away, two miles away, and then rushing over the railroad tracks. Folks ran to a position between the fire and the church. They poured water and beat at the flames with blankets.

When the fire reached the end of the wheat field, the blankets and buckets stopped it. The firemen sprayed water on the side and roof of the church. The folks walked around the edge stomping out smoldering piles of stubble.

Then the people gathered, and plenty of beer made the rounds. The folks had to tell and retell the events. Soon the fire truck and the relatives left Wann. I snuck behind our house to wait for the punishment.

Dad's strap stung across the back of my guilty little Washburn butt. It stung across the back of my legs. I cried before the first strike. At the end I hoped that Mom hadn't heard. I felt that each sting of pain released more guilt, each sting dissolved more flame pictures, and more matches were never to be in my hands again. In the end, people had saved the church, and in a strange way of thinking, salvation through punishment had saved me.

As I lay in bed that night, I felt I had paid the price for redemption. I felt sorry that my actions caused such damage. I also felt that, in the morning, I could get on with my life. I didn't blame Dad for my punishment. If he hadn't punished me, I think I would have carried too much guilt into my future.

A week after the fire incident, Dad made an announcement.

"You two oldest are going to work. Should keep your butts out of trouble. Got you jobs exercising race horses. Be ready to go by six tomorrow morning."

Of course I was pissed. Why didn't he get himself a job? My ideal conduct was lots of playtime and little work. All I could do was pout to show off my lousy attitude.

He gave me a hard look. "I don't want anyone making a fuss or else."

It was tough getting my head ready that early. I tried to endure the motion of a moving car. My stomach twisted when Dad took a corner or jumped the car over a bump in an intersection. Norman lay down in the back seat. I sat up front with Dad because sometimes that helped.

After ten minutes, "Dad, I've got to puke."

"Dammit, it's all in your head. Roll down the window. Stick your head out for fresh air."

I did what he said. When my stomach churned up into my mouth, I experienced a case of dry heaves. Dad cussed, pulled over, and stopped. He walked around to see if I had puked on his car. I sat back, my stomach felt better, my head felt light. Once Dad reached Ashland and drove onto Highway 6, the ride was smoother. He parked near the horse barns at the state fairgrounds in Lincoln.

"Get a donut and a glass of milk."

We walked behind him to a small white building, the Horseman's Café. We climbed up on the counter stools next to him. The odors assaulted my sensitive nose. Hot coffee, horse sweat, manure, cigarette smoke and frying bacon grease.

Dad ordered coffee and began to read the form. We had a glass of milk and one glazed donut. After that, my stomach felt great. When Dad won money we could get an extra donut.

Next, Dad walked us over to the horse barns. We walked around puddles of muddy water and horse urine. If it rained and the piles were soggy, then the smell was awful.

Dad had an arrangement with a few horse trainers. He left us with Vernon "the jock" Grauerholz. Vernon used to be a jockey until he gained too much weight. He stood a little taller than Norman. By this time, we knew what jockeys looked like, so we didn't stare at him. His clothes were dirty and smelled of beer, and he wore one of those caps with a little bill, the kind I saw on rich men's heads.

Bushy whiskers covered Vernon's chin. His pants, held up by a black belt, seemed high on his belly. I could see that his red socks and black shoes had patches of dry horse manure stuck on them.

The jock watched Dad walk away and then he growled at us.

"Saw you boys in the diner. How'd you like them fat cakes?"

I took a half step back, but Norman spoke up.

"What's fat cakes?"

"Whats you ate in there. What'll you call 'em?"

"You mean donuts?"

Vernon thought on that for a second.

"Weren't no nuts in them, were there?"

Norman shook his head and replied, "Where's the horses?"

"That's Vernon's worry, not yourn. Say, you boys ever hear this? Listen, listen the cat is apissin', where, where, under the chair, quick, quick, get the gun, oh shit, he's all done."

I stood staring at Vernon. Norman spoke up. "Nah, never heard it."

I knew both of us had committed the verse to memory. The next chance we had, we would practice it.

"Aw hell," Vernon said, "I reckon you boys a couple of rookies. Probably don't even know what do to with a girl. Probably never been with one. Old Vernon here, I could tell you a lot about 'em. Ever seen the girl magazines?"

"What horses do we walk?" Norman asked.

"Alrighty, ready to work, eh? Here's the rules. Count the laps around the barn. Do thirty with each horse. Don't get close to other horses. Always walk on the left side. Now watch this."

He hooked a black leather strap onto the halter of the nearest horse. Then he opened the stall door and led the horse outside.

Vernon pointed to me, "You take Mr. Baker. I reckon he's gentle enough for you."

I had chased chickens, whipped hogs with a yardstick, yanked calves around with a rope on their halter, but I had never been around horses. They were too large. I was afraid their large foot would come down on my shoe. I wished I owned a pair of steel-tipped shoes like old man Everman had been selling.

Vernon began to walk Mr. Baker on the path around the horse barn. I followed him until he gave me the lead strap. Thank the Lord the horse could have walked by himself. Vernon followed me around once then he got a horse out for Norman.

Around and around I walked Mr. Baker. I had to stop him twice to let other horses out of their stalls. I began to gawk around. Pony boys on horses trotted by on their way to the track for exercises. I lost count of the laps, so I guessed about thirty, and then turned Mr. Baker back to Vernon.

"Okay," he said, "now walk him into his stall. Turn him around until he's facing out. Unhook the strap. Don't let him run out."

While I walked the horse, Vernon had cleaned out the stall and tossed in fresh straw. My confidence grew so that the next two horses were easy to handle. After two hours, Norman and I had walked three horses each. They had funny names like Mean Streak, Mud Ball, and Darlla Nay.

We looked for Dad but couldn't see him. We walked over to a two-stall batting cage. For a quarter, a machine would throw baseballs at us. A rough-looking boy was running it. He came over when he saw us and said a few words to Norman. Norman smarted back to him.

Hell, I thought, *Norm's going to fight*. That kid acted like something was wrong with him. I didn't know what his problem was; maybe he didn't belong to a family as we did. He became friendlier when he realized he couldn't scare Norman.

Dad appeared, said it was time to go.

"You get fifty cents for each horse you walk. I'll collect your money at the end of the week. No races today, we're going home."

I slept on the way back to Wann. It was late afternoon when we arrived. I didn't feel like playing. I was a working boy.

For supper Mom had a surprise. She cooked a batch of pancakes. Then she brought out a small tin of syrup. Shaped like a log cabin, the syrup tin had a screw top that represented the chimney. The words, Log Cabin Syrup, appeared on the side.

When I saw that little cabin, I knew I had to have it as a toy.

"Mom, can I have that tin when it's empty?"

"No way," Mickey said, "it's mine. Already asked."

So once again a fight started, one I knew I couldn't win. I went to bed pissed off. Mom said she would clean it up when it was empty, and all of us could play with it.

The next month of summer vacation went like that. Some mornings Dad said the barns didn't want us. Some days, the whole family went early, and spent the day at the racetrack. Dad gave Norman and me a few dollars bills at the end of each week.

"Now you boys can pay your way into the picture show on Saturday night. Buy your own soda pop and popcorn. Save some to buy your school shoes."

I didn't keep track of how much I earned each week. Once I told Dad we should have a dollar more, and he got pissed.

"One owner didn't pay." That was all he said.

Finally, the last day of walking horses arrived. By this time we had picked other favorite horses, but Mr. Baker remained my preferred. We figured we had better like Hold On Harry due to our Dad's name. Our other favorites were Line Dancer, Red Caboose, and Born Loser who was anything but.

When we finished our last job, Vernon told us to follow him. We went to the end of a horse barn where Vernon unlocked a stall door. I looked in. A number of medicine jars sat on shelves. A strong whiff of Sloan's Liniment cleared out my head.

When we walked in, I realized this was where he lived. The floor didn't have straw on it; a faded piece of blue carpet covered the dirt base. There was a cot in one corner and a high cupboard with no shelves. A few of his clothes were hanging inside it.

"Here's one of those girly magazines," Vernon said, "I reckon you boys can pay a dollar for it."

He pulled a magazine from under his cot. I looked around to make sure Dad didn't walk in on us.

Norman said, "Let's see some pictures."

"I reckon not. Nothing free, you boys old enough to know that."

Norman dug in his pocket for change. Then he turned toward me.

"Loan me a quarter. Pay you back when we get home."

Since I had a job, I did carry money with me. So I gave Norman a quarter, he got the magazine, and we told Vernon goodbye. I had about seven one dollar bills after our final payment.

In our back bedroom, there was one set of drawers. Each boy had one drawer for his clothes. I hid my bills under socks in the back. Even though I felt richer than ever, Mom wouldn't let us spurge daily at the store. One bottle of soda pop and five cents worth of candy per day was the limit.

Soon after Norman told Mom he wanted a crew-cut haircut.

"Dad can't do it. He doesn't have the right clippers. All the Ashland boys have crew-cuts."

I said, "Dad isn't here long enough to cut all our hair."

"I'll ask," Mom said, and soon Norman and I were sitting in a barber chair in Ashland. We paid the fifty cents that Dad gave us. Now we were in a style that put us ahead of the Wann farm boys.

CHAPTER FOURTEEN

1951

When the next church event happened, I forgot about looking at Norman's magazine, and I almost forgot about my stash of money.

Sometimes Mom made us sing in the youth choir which was usually made up of four Washburn boys.

Toward the middle of August, Mom made the announcement.

I've signed you all up to be baptized."

Well hell, that caused an uproar.

"What the hell for?" I blurted out.

"Why do we have to do it?"

"Who's going to baptize us?'

"When is it?"

Thank the Lord Mom pretended she didn't hear me. I couldn't believe that when my soul needed salvation, I cussed out loud. My ways clearly needed mended.

Once we had attended the Christian Church in Ashland to see a cousin baptized. There was a tank of water up front behind a curtain. When the curtain opened, the minister said a few words, and then tipped our cousin backwards into the water. That was all I knew about baptisms.

Next, we found out our baptism wasn't going to be ordinary. There would not be a confirmation class, no sprinkling of holy water, no touching of hands to our heads.

This arrangement was totally out of the Bible. All God's children would gather at the Wann sandpit. For crying out loud! The sandpit with its discolored water and tadpoles swimming around the edge? The sandpit where pastured cows lived and you had to be careful of the cow pies when you walked there?

Yes, that was the idea. Dad took off for Sportsman Park in Chicago. On Sunday Mom outfitted us in new white shirts and cheap slacks. We tucked a hankie into our back pockets for our nose. Fifteen kids were to receive the blessing of sandpit water.

When the first farm cars parked in front of the store, Mom led us out of the house. A line of people walked from the store, over the railroad tracks, across Grandpa's tomato field, and through a gate that a farmer had opened. I was nervous since I had reached the age where I didn't want to be embarrassed in front of others.

The congregation stood at the edge of the sandpit and sang hymns. "Just as I am" and "We Are Climbing Jacob's Ladder". My brothers and I weren't climbing; we were wading into murky water. I heard farm wives declare, "May the Lord have mercy."

The elders pounded stakes into the water and connected them with a rope. The Minister, Archer Smith, spoke a few words and then waded out until the water came up to his waist.

One at a time we held onto the rope and walked into the lukewarm water. Norman was the first boy. He handed his hankie to the minister who said a few words. The minister placed the hankie over Norman's mouth and nose, dunked him backwards, and then raised him up. I took my turn, but my mind quavered. The crowd of witnesses lifted up their voices with "Be Thou My Vision."

Finally, we joined in a group prayer. Then all traipsed back over the pasture, over the tracks after we waited for a freight train, and then the farmers drove their saved kids home. Going to bed that night, I reflected on what caused my head problem.

I knew that once we spoke our faith our souls were "saved". I wasn't sure what a soul was, but Mom felt it was essential. Therefore, that part felt religious, and a good thing to have happened. However, something took my mind away from being one hundred percent soulful in nature. I gained full knowledge that I was a sinner during the ceremony.

One of the older farm girls was in front of Norman. When the minister raised her up, her white shirt was soaked. I looked and saw through her shirt. Before, I had not spent much time being curious about that. I was totally into games, books, and sports. I couldn't help it. I wanted to see more, so I stared at her until she passed by.

I wondered if I could blame the devil for the temptation. Saved by grace the minister said. Then my eyes opened to sin as my human nature took over. Before I fell into an uneasy sleep, I tried to recall the picture of what I had seen. The mysteries of human desire came into my heart, but ignorance of what it all meant came into my mind. For me, life wasn't getting any easier.

The nightly prayer didn't give me any comfort. "Now I lay me down to sleep, I pray the Lord my soul to keep, and if I die before I wake, I pray the Lord my soul to take."

"Die before I wake" was as confusing to me as my soul saved by grace.

My life changed then. Transgressions happened; I repented. Then, like a floating dead fish in the sand pits, the picture of the farm girl came to mind unbidden, but with visual stimulation.

Grandma gave us clip-on ties as a baptism present. Therefore, white shirts with ties became our Sunday school attire. We lined up for another Washburn boys' black and white photo. We looked innocent, not like kids who would cause their mother to shed tears.

Shortly thereafter, Mom announced a plan to encourage us to behave.

"I'm putting all the pennies from change in a jar. Even the ones we get from selling race programs. Here's a chart where you get a mark when you misbehave. The one with the least marks gets the money."

Mickey and I got into a fight and received the first marks. I was pissed, acted as if I didn't care. Pennies couldn't change our behavior. In the end she divided the loot, and when it hit our hands the race was on to the store.

Then school began. Norman and I sat in the big room, grades five through eight. Mickey and Kenny in the little room, grades one though four.

A week later I remembered that I was going to buy Mom an early Christmas present before I wasted my money. Since I had extra cash, I planned to get the present the next Saturday night in Ashland. There was a five and dime variety store as well as Harris's Drug Store. Both of them had lots of knickknacks and doodads. Figured I could pick out something, but I had no idea what.

When I opened my drawer and lifted a pair of socks to retrieve my stash, I thought someone had played a trick on me. Then I moved all my clothes around, searched for my dollars bills. Finally, I felt sick when I realized all of my savings were gone.

"Mom, have you seen my money? Sure I left it in the bottom of my drawer."

Now Mom was always there for us boys. She raised us, fed us, clothed us, had us baptized. I would never suspect her of doing wrong concerning her boys. Yet, when I asked that question, she turned away, wouldn't look at me. I couldn't remember a time when she acted strange, unless some crucial event was approaching.

Her back to me, she began ironing clothes. "No, haven't seen it. You sure you saved any?"

"Am sure I had seven dollars in my drawer."

She didn't answer. At that moment, I knew what had happened. Most of the time she was loyal to her husband. When he lost, she blamed it on bad luck. She knew I had that money; she put my socks and shorts away.

However, there was no way I could accuse Dad. He would lose his temper and beat the hell out of me for even suggesting it. Mom probably told him. He snitched it, thinking he would win and replace it. He would hit that lick he was always talking about. Never, dammit, never did he return it.

I didn't feel too happy about myself. I had no guts, no spine, and a yellow stripe down my back. Why didn't I speak up to him? It wasn't long before I realized I couldn't connect with any adult. From a young age, I had recognized him as the authority figure. I figured all adults would order me around as he did.

I grew up with virtually nothing. Now I was back to zero. How badly I wished I could distance myself from him. Even his jokes and his bullshit had become too obvious. *Just wait*, I thought, *just wait*.

Two days later I was spending time alone at dusk. I wandered behind the house. Just then, I felt a stillness in the air. I looked around, and then stuck my head in the shed door.

A movement up high caught my eye. There was a gray snake moving along the rafters. I froze. I couldn't see its head. Then I thought it must be a tail. Maybe a rat's tail. A part of the body moved lower. I ran for the house.

I grabbed my BB gun and gave it a pump. Norman looked up from the table.

"Norm. Quick. A rat."

I ran back to the shed and stepped inside. I felt Norman charge in behind me.

"Up there." I pointed my gun.

The gray tail was still waving along the rafters. When part of the body lowered I took aim and pulled the trigger. The body and the tail didn't change position. I heard the ping of the bb ricocheting off the walls. Then I heard Norman yelp.

I turned and saw him put his hand under his right eye. Blood began to run down his face.

"Thanks a hell of a lot. You dumb ass. Can't you see it's a cobweb?"

I looked closer, walked over, and stuck the gun's barrel into the dusty cobweb. Evidently, too many things scared me. Norman hustled to the pump and washed the blood off his face. We walked into the house.

"Mom, I need a Band-Aid."

"How'd that happen?"

Norman looked at me and then said, "A tree branch stuck me."

I was glad he didn't snitch on me. And I thought this: I have a scar between my eyes from him breaking a glass. Now he'll have a scar because of my foolishness. I was scared during a dream that night because a gray snake was chasing me.

At the end of summer Dad bought a race horse. He had been on a roll, so we were enjoying the boom time.

"Got me a horse, boys. Name is Tsuluk. Now watch the money pile up."

Sure, I thought. Roll the dice, deal the cards, and spin the wheel. Here we go again. However, I couldn't help but feel optimistic. Maybe this time he would hit a lick.

Dad spent his surplus on the horse and a stall and feed. He paid a trainer to get the horse ready.

One night with windows and doors closed, Dad educated us.

"Listen boys. This horse can run. But we got to use our heads. Here's what I aim to do. Tell the jockey to hold him back the first two times he runs. By the third time, the odds will be up and the payoff higher. We unload all our money on him to win."

Mom asked, "Is that legal?"

"Hell yes. You kidding me? Everybody does it. The jock has to be smart and not let on what he doing, that's all."

Mom said, "Hope this isn't another one of your rabbit pens."

I guessed Dad was too excited to get pissed off about that comment. Our family was riding the roller coaster of happiness all the way to the top. The next day he gave us five cents each and told us to get a bottle of soda pop.

"Drink it at the store. Stay away for a half hour."

The first two times the horse ran everything worked. He came in sixth the first race and fifth the next. Dad entered his horse in the seventh race on the last day of the meet in Lincoln. The family made the trip.

"Norman and Warren, I know you guys got some spending money. Give me a dollar each. I'll buy you a two-dollar ticket to win."

We were too nervous to stand still. We ran around, picked up tickets, and watched the races. Grandma, Grandpa, Wendell, and Arlene arrived. Wendell was home on leave. Mom chewed her gum faster as the seventh race neared.

Grandpa took us boys down to the paddock before the big race. Dad had dressed up and was inside. He gave the jockey last-minute instructions. The horses walked out at the sound of the bugle. I had to pee so bad, I ran to the toilet.

As the horses warmed up, the clan gathered in the center of the grandstand.

Dad said, "When they take the winner's picture, the owner gets in it. I can take one with me. Who wants to go?"

I thought it wouldn't be one of us kids. Grandma gave her warning, "Don't count your chickens before they hatch."

Mom held a ticket in her hand. It was considered bad luck to talk about who you bet on and how much. Dad quit joking. Finally, the horses approached the starting gate.

I held my breath as the commands echoed around the grandstand. "They're at the gate." A hush settled over the crowd. Then the bell clanged, and the announcer's "They're off!"

Dad's horse had drawn the number five post position. He charged out of the gate with knees high and tail streaming out. As they raced in front of the grandstand, he had a one length lead. The jockey eased him over to the rail.

I stood frozen. The relatives screamed, jumped, and beat each other with their programs. Around the first curve, number five dashed. He stretched out his lead to three lengths. I felt like my ears would pop. I watched the horses, but felt as if I were standing in a vacuum with a continuous howl surrounding me.

Across the track the horses raced down the backstretch. As they curved around the rail heading into the stretch, it seemed as if number five faltered a bit. Two horses had closed the gap. I held my breath.

As they neared the edge of the grandstand, the two horses pulled alongside Dad's horse. To the wire they raced. A sign showing 'photo finish' flashed on the tote board. It didn't look like number five had won.

Dad said, "Damn trainer didn't have him in shape."

As another howl erupted from the crowd, I heard Dad cuss,

"Damn it all to hell. I'm through with this race track."

The racing stewards picked number five to show. Dad hustled down the steps.

Grandpa said, "Maybe he's going to protest."

Wendell and Arlene tore up their tickets and threw them down. They left without talking. Later we learned they were so angry they wouldn't ride home with anyone. They hitched a ride on Highway 6 and then Sam picked them up in Ashland. Sam held a two dollar show ticket, so he got his money back plus a couple more since the odds were high.

The trip back was quiet. Nobody asked Dad if we were going to play 'who can see the Wann elevator first' game. The next week Dad took his horse to the races at Columbus where Tsuluk won his first two races. Dad made a little purse money, and he made a lot on his bets. However, he didn't talk about it. He paid Grandpa what he owned for past debts and past rents. Then he sold the horse. He got ready to go south to Hot Springs, Arkansas, for the horse races at Oaklawn Park.

That school year was one of my worst ever. The annual school picnic took place after the last school day. Men played baseball while the women filled long tables with pot-luck food. Cakes, pies, and ice cream were on hand for dessert. After the dinner, us school kids had races by the class we were in. I liked to win.

As my class lined up, my nerves reached a peak as I looked at my classmates. On the go, we raced to the finish line. Who would have ever thought Judy Veskerna could run fast enough to beat me? Afterwards, I felt so sorry for myself, I almost cried. When Uncle Larry asked me how I did I told him.

He patted my shoulder and said, "Just take it like a man."

I beat Judy the next two years but the shame surfaced every time I though about it.

CHAPTER FIFTEEN

1952

Dad became a jockey agent at a race track in Cleveland, Ohio, during the summer of '52. Aunt Aloha told us Ohio was the only state that was high in the middle and round on both ends. She laughed when I couldn't see the joke.

We picked strawberries, played baseball games, and did chores. We sat on the bench in front of the store and watched for any car, truck, or train to go by. I treasured my bottle of soda with the red and yellow logo, Royal Crown Cola. Once Grandma gave us a cold bottle of chocolate milk. It was five cents also, but you had to shake it first since chocolate had settled to the bottom.

Dad called. Mom talked in hushed tones. Something was going on. Mom cooked pancakes for Sunday dinner. She fried hamburgers to eat with our pancakes. *A new and satisfying surprise*, I thought, and then Grandma walked in.

"Boys, I made you a mincemeat pie."

What the heck was that? I loved pies, but the words 'meat and pie' didn't go together. It was a strange looking combination and there was no way I was going to taste it. When Grandma turned her back, I shoveled mine onto Mickey's plate. He loved it. Both adults were acting mysteriously, so I began to pay attention. Mom told us to sit down.

"Your dad rented a furnished house in Cleveland. We're going to live there for the summer."

"Does it have an indoor toilet?"

"How do we get there?"

"Do some of us get bedrooms?"

Then I heard the best news of all.

"On Tuesday your Grandpa will drive us to the Ashland depot. We'll ride a train to Chicago. Your dad will pick us up."

My most favorite Christmas present had been a wind-up locomotive which pulled two boxcars and a caboose. It ran around a small circle of tracks while shooting sparks out from the engine. But now, to ride on a real train was beyond belief. We had studied God and his tender mercies in our Sunday school class. Now I believed.

Despite my faith as a child's, fear and doubts took over my mind. I knew something would change. I wished I had a lucky pen like Dad's to fight off any jinx.

We packed three suitcases of clothes. Grandpa drove over Tuesday morning and we loaded up. I heard Mom say to Sam, "We could have left two hours earlier. But our train goes faster and doesn't stop as much."

Wow, didn't she know that would be what we wanted. A longer train ride. It was just a minor disappointment, easily forgotten as we walked into the Ashland depot.

Then I worried that our train would be delayed causing us to return to Wann. However, right on time the black engine pulled into the station. Mom held us back from rushing onto the tracks before it stopped.

"Mom, is it the Denver Zephyr?"

"Don't know. Grab your sacks. This is our car."

We told Grandpa goodbye, he told us to stay out of trouble. I stared at the enormous locomotive, one coal car, one mail car, and three dark green passenger cars. I couldn't believe we had done anything to deserve this.

We grabbed our lunch sacks and stepped up into a passenger car. Only a few people were there, so we could sit wherever we wanted on the dusty, padded seats. I switched three times. A few minutes later and a couple short blasts of a whistle, our train began to move. Goodbye Wann, goodbye Ashland, goodbye Nebraska.

It was scary crossing the bridge over the Platte River. All I could see was water below my window and out the other window. When we pulled into Omaha, there was a thirty minute stop. Norman and I stepped out of our car and stood by the steps. I held on to the railing. He wanted to get off and explore the Omaha depot, but I was too scared.

The conductor herded us back, "All board," he hollered and picked up his wooden footstool. We hustled back to our seats. Another long river bridge crossed the Missouri River.

Mom took us to the end of the car where two small tables sat between seats. We opened our sacks and ate pieces of fried chicken. I made the mistake of sitting facing the wrong direction. Something about seeing the countryside flashing backwards made my head dizzy. Had to switch seats to calm down a bit.

The train kept moving at a speedy rate. We saw objects we had never seen before. Cities bigger than Lincoln. Huge power plants. Freight trains lined up in railroad yards. Vast piles of materials we had no name for. *What a lucky break for us*, I thought. All that we saw opened our eyes to one strange world after another.

It felt important to coast into a town and look ahead at the flashing red lights which caused cars to stop for us. Norman and I grew braver as the train stopped at each depot. We stood at the end of the car and talked to the conductor.

When we climbed down, we stayed close to our car. The first call of "all board" we jumped back up the steps.

When nightfall came, all we could see was moving lights. Our train coasted into the station in Chicago. We were no longer outside; there was a roof overhead.

My legs felt shaky climbing down the steps. Mickey and Kenny saw Dad in the distance, yelled at him, and started to run.

"Stop! Stop!" Mom yelled. They had to cross railroad tracks where other trains were coming and going. Dad cussed at them a bit and then collected us, suitcases were loaded in the trunk, and off he drove into the traffic and city lights.

I fell asleep. Later when I woke up I looked out and saw nothing but street and building lights.

"Mom, what town are we in?"

"We're still in Chicago."

I couldn't believe it. I must have slept for half an hour. If you drove by Wann and blinked, you wouldn't even see the village.

In the dark of night, Dad stopped in Ohio. We trooped into a motel room and barely got our clothes off before we fell asleep. The next day's drive wasn't as fun as the train ride. Four boys cooped up in the hot back seat made for some restless times.

On a bright June afternoon, Dad stopped in front of a two-story white house. For us boys, it was a castle. It had a genuine upstairs with bedrooms and one indoor toilet. Norman and I slept in a bedroom on a real bed.

We explored every room in the house. Outside the house, we jogged around on the grass lawn. We were going to live in a different world.

We adjusted to life in a city. In Wann, a four-year couldn't get lost. But here, with houses everywhere, actual sidewalks and paved streets, it was enough to make us feel misplaced. Dad left early every morning for the race track.

We didn't hike down streets--too many people and cars. One block down from our house the sidewalk ended. A forest with tall trees, thick vines, and depressed gullies began there. We went exploring in it every day.

We followed trails until we felt we were getting too far away. The air felt heavy, making it difficult to breathe at times. Moldy leaves gave out a musty smell as we kicked them. Scratchy vines and low branches swept past our bare arms. We walked into swarms of mosquitoes.

One afternoon we hiked a long time down a hollow gully. The air was still and we were sweating. We curved around a bend and stopped suddenly. There a man stood, looking at us. I couldn't guess his age, younger than Dad I thought.

"You guys watching out for poisonous snakes? You look like a bunch of hayseeds."

He wore glasses and his head appeared odd shaped, like a bullet. He stuck it forward when he talked. We stared at him.

"Just hiking," Norman said.

"You ought to carry sticks. Snakes hereabouts look like dead leaves. Some hang on branches real quiet like."

When we had no answer, he continued, "Me, I got me an Arkansaw toothpick. Case any snake comes after me." He pulled a long knife out of his belt.

I yanked on Norman's arm, "Let's go back now. We've been gone long enough."

We turned and then we heard him, "Didn't mean to give you hicks ants in your pants."

We began to jog.

We met other kids. Boys and girls walked down our block to play and visit. A brother and sister hung out with us. The girl was my age. I thought she was cute. That was as far as my thoughts went.

Romance was something forward in my future. She was a tomboy. I didn't think that surprising since the Wann farm girls were tomboys. They could swing a bat, catch a baseball, and run almost as fast as the Wann boys.

What I couldn't get over was her name--Peanuts. That was the only name she went by. Never knew her real name. Peanuts and her brother would play the usual games like tag and kick the can. They wouldn't explore in the forest with us, however.

After we had lived there for a while, Mom had another surprise.

"We're going shopping tomorrow in downtown Cleveland. Have to take a bus to get there. If we have time, maybe we'll see a movie matinee."

The next day we wore clean clothes. We had to walk seven blocks to a bus stop. It was a thirty minute ride to downtown and not much fun. Too many people on the bus and too much stale air. We stayed close to Mom once we left the bus. Tall buildings, people of every color, and we had to be careful crossing a street. In Wann we walked down the middle of the roads.

When we walked into a department store, I looked ahead and saw doors at the other end. "Mom, look. This store is a block long. We can go out by another door."

Even in Lincoln you went in a store by one door and came out the same door. Mom bought us a hamburger in a corner restaurant. We shared a large basket of French fries. *Dad must have done well at the races to pay for these expenses*, I thought.

As promised, we went to an afternoon movie, Mighty Joe Young. It was an older one, brought back for matinees. It had an enormous gorilla chasing people in a big city, just like King Kong. Sometimes lions broke out and ran wild. Not as good as the first gorilla movie I had seen.

Once more that summer we took the bus downtown for shopping and a movie. I thought our Wann make-up games were going to seem tame when we returned. Sometimes I thought Peanuts was too bossy. Once she called me a beanpole which got my dopper down.

On the way home from one of our hikes, I developed a strong itch between my legs. "Scratch where it itches," was a Wann saying so that's what I did. Didn't seem to help. When I went into the bathroom, I pulled my jeans down and examined my inner legs.

Two black dots were causing the itch, one on the inside of each leg. *What terror of hell is this*, I thought. My privates, being private, it took a lot of guts for me to show Mom.

"I've got a problem," I told her. I pulled down my jeans and pointed.

She bent over to inspect my legs and said, "You've got ticks."

She flicked a fingernail under each and pulled them off. They had little wiggly feet. Then she flushed them down the stool.

"Put some mercurochrome on the bites," she said. "You boys need to check your bodies every day if you're going to play down there."

I wasn't sure I wanted to explore the forest anymore. Too many strange happenings. Our summer vacation was mostly pure vanilla with only a few incidents to ruin a trip to a magic kingdom. However, Dad disappointed us in the middle of summer.

Since we had graduated from bib overalls to blue jeans, we considered ourselves as top notch balls of fire. Showing off in the neighborhood, wearing our white T-shirts and blue jeans made us appear as normal kids. However, soon we noticed that our clothes weren't the same style as the other kids'.

What they wore were shorts. Usually they were tan in color and ended above the knees, and everyone had brown legs. We scouted this situation out and then considered our lily white legs. We began our begging campaign with Mom.

"Can't we have shorts like the other kids?"

"Ask your Dad."

That wasn't good news. He was going through another bad luck streak. He was in a terrible mood, not too concerned whether or not his sons were in style. Mom took up our cause.

"Maybe next week you'll do better. Then see about the shorts."

Finally, he relented and shopped for our shorts. Regular ones like the other kids' were too expensive. He brought home men's boxer shorts and told us, "By damn you better wear them after I spent all that money." We were sick.

The shorts didn't button at the waist. They had an elastic band to keep them up. They were white or blue with stripes or solid red or covered with green dots. And worst of all, they didn't fit snug. They ballooned up when we tried them on.

We tried to slip out the next morning in our costumes. Right before we snuck into the trees, some nosy kid yelled, "Hey, you got your dad's shorts on?" To be expected, Norman told him to shut up. Then they got into a wrestling match on the ground.

We never wore them again. I don't know what happened to those shorts, but they sure as heck didn't make the trip back to Wann. We couldn't wear them in Wann anyway. We played on our knees in the sand or tall weeds. Blue jeans worked better then. I don't think Dad ever mentioned them again either.

Early in August, we packed our clothes for the trip home. Peanuts showed up the night before to give Norman and me a going away present.

"Here's something to send you away."

It was a small white package with the words SEN-SEN on the cover.

"What is it?" I asked.

"It's SEN-SEN to send you, get it?"

I never knew what that dizzy girl was thinking.

"Try some."

We opened the packages. Inside were small black squares. I placed a couple on my tongue. They had a strong licorice taste, burned just a little.

Peanuts said, "Why don't you send a postcard from Nebraska?"

"Sure and thanks for the present."

Like I'm going to spend a coin on a postcard, when I could buy a cold bottle of soda pop with it. She must have been out of her mind.

On the drive home, Dad had me sit up front at times so I wouldn't get motion sickness. Otherwise, the back seat felt cramped. It was sweaty and we crabbed at each other. We tried to occupy our minds and tried to sleep.

Our only stops were for gas, bathroom, and hamburgers and milk. Dad didn't stop for a motel. On through the night he drove. By the time we drove passed Omaha I could see a faint outline of pink sky in the east.

Early that morning we drove into Wann. It looked as if we had never left. The village was quiet, no movement. Dad drove up to the bank building and we piled out. Inside, it smelled musty. We had to prime the pump with water from Grandpa's to get it working.

Norman and I wandered over to the school grounds. We sat and talked about Cleveland. It seemed so far away, and yet our vacation stuck firm in our memories, like a dream that's hard to forget.

Grandpa came over for a visit that night.

"No more movies in Ashland. The Neu Theatre burned down while you were gone."

Damn, that was awful news. I had begun to take an interest in the town girls. When Norman and his friends visited with them, the scene looked like fun. I liked the girls who smiled. However, in my mind girls were too mysterious. With guys, it was let's play games. Girls' eyes seemed to hide secrets and exciting mysteries.

CHAPTER SIXTEEN

1952

Hard times struck the family all fall and winter of 1952. Christmas approached with no end in sight of our rotten luck. When used Christmas paper covered our presents it didn't bother us. Dad ordered us to unwrap the paper carefully. Mom folded it and saved it for the next Christmas.

"Listen." Norman whispered. Mom and Dad were in bed, talking.

We heard Mom say, "Boys are used to not having a Christmas tree, but they've got to have a present."

It was hard to lie still after that. Maybe, just maybe we would get a Christmas present. Our building was too small for a tree anyway.

Mom was feisty at times, and I loved her because she tended to her four boys like a mother hen. If she ever showed anger, it was always against Dad and his ways.

We heard Dad say, "Got no choice. Them two hogs got to go. I'm out of luck at the horse races."

Mom was silent for a while.

"How you going to haul 'em?"

"Get Dad's truck in the morning. See if Larry can help. Two oldest boys can go too. Little work won't hurt them."

We heard no more. I felt excited for the chance of a present, but unhappy about having to go out in the cold and snow. Norm and I had already figured out the Santa Claus and Tooth Fairy scheme.

I thought of last year's Christmas. Dad had a lucky streak. He handed us a Sears Roebuck catalog and told us to pick out one present, up to five dollars.

The four days leading up to our decisions were nerve racking. I narrowed my selection to fifty green army men or a cowboy hat and holster set with two pistols. Finally, I picked the cowboy outfit.

When I woke the next morning, I pulled on my clothes and a jacket to go take my turn in the outhouse. It was already snowing. A bitter wind came through the jacket. I hoped Dad had forgotten about making Norman and me go with him. I didn't have the inclination to suffer the cold to prove anything to anyone. I would rather stick by the stove reading my Roy Rogers book.

Mom cooked Dad's favorite breakfast, poached eggs on a piece of wet toast. I could barely stomach that mixture. I was stirring it around in my bowl when Dad announced, "Norman and Warren, get ready. Help me load those two hogs. Ride along to Ashland."

Damn, I knew then it was going to be a miserable day. However, we might end up with a Christmas present. That thought kept me going.

"Come here boys," Mom said, "it's zero outside. Put these catalog pages inside your overshoes."

She pulled down our earflaps; zipped up our jackets, and made sure we had gloves. After we had pulled overshoes on, she tore pages out of the Sears catalog and stuffed them in to keep our feet warm.

Dad flipped a white diaper over his head and tied it under his chin. Then he placed his hat over it. He tucked his blue corduroy pant legs into his overshoes.

Uncle Larry walked in. "I've got the truck. Dad says it'll need gas before we head home."

As I walked out, I looked at Mick and Ken. They got to stay home with Mom; they got to stay warm. I hoped they had to wash and dry the dishes.

Before Dad led us outside, Mom told him to spend some pig money on groceries.

"We're out of milk, bread, and eggs."

Outside, we walked back to the pen as Larry drove the truck next to the fence.

"Boys, toss some straw and a couple of corn scoops in the truck."

We carried two loads of straw and spread it out. By the time we crawled inside with the scoops, Larry and Dad had caught one hog and shoved it in behind us.

"Warren, use the scoop. Keep the damn thing away from the driver's seat. Norman, shut the door. When I knock on it, open up, but don't let this hog out."

Larry left the truck running so we warmed up. The pig grunted and sniffed at the straw. Then Dad pounded on the back door. When Norman opened it, the first pig shot past him and jumped out.

"Dammit!" Dad yelled. "Grab him!"

Larry tossed the second hog into the truck and began to run

through the snow with Norman close behind. Dad slammed the door shut. I grabbed the scoop and pointed it toward the hog since the beady look in his eyes scared me. He snorted, sniffed the straw, and then plopped down.

I opened the front door to get a better look at the action. The free hog scooted down the road with Jigger giving chase and nipping at the hog's hind legs.

I thought I should help by backing up the truck. Norman and I had sat in Dad's old cars before. He showed me where the clutch was and the foot feed. Also, how the gear stick worked. I slid into the driver's seat and thought if I could get the truck moving, I would steer it back on the road in a straight line. If I strained hard enough, my feet could reach the pedals.

The gear stick felt loose, so I pushed down on the clutch with my left foot. I moved the stick over to the left, then up to where I thought reverse would be. I pressed halfway down on the foot feed and let up on the clutch. The truck lurched backwards with jerking motions.

Suddenly Larry pounded on the side window and yelled, "Stop! Stop! You're in the ditch!"

I let up on the clutch and the foot feed. The truck gave a violent lurch and shut off. Dad cussed as he opened the back door. They shoved in the escaped pig and slammed the door shut. I moved back into the straw before Dad got in and started up on me.

"If this truck doesn't start and if I can't get it out of the ditch, you're getting the belt to your butt! You hear me?"

I nodded. Thankfully, the truck started. Dad tromped down on the clutch, shifted the gear, goosed the foot feed, and blasted the truck out of the ditch and down the road past the store. The hogs, Norman, and I bounced around, but we didn't laugh in case we pissed off Dad a little more.

The Ashland sales barn was seven miles away. Larry sat in the passenger seat, Norman and I sat down in the straw. We held a scoop and kept an eye on the hogs.

Dad drove steadily since small drifts were building up across the gravel road. After a few minutes, Norman began to giggle and pointed at one of the hogs. I looked at it and thought it was taking a leak.

Just then Norman hollered, "Dad! One of them has the shits back here!"

"Oh hell, throw some straw over it. Stop it from stinking. Larry, roll down your window. It's getting a little in-tense up here." They started to laugh.

"Norman. Watch your cussing. Next time it's the yardstick."

My stomach began to react. A dizzy feeling in my head and a bubble in my gut started a chain reaction. The truck motion and the pee and poop smell did me in.

I climbed between Dad and Larry. "Dad, I've got to puke."

He slowed the truck. "Larry, stick his head out your door."

Larry opened his door, grabbed me, and pulled me toward it. I upchucked the poached egg and toast. Dad stopped the truck. A few spurts and I was done. Feeling light-headed, I crawled back to the straw.

"Look. There's Ashland," Larry said.

We looked through the snow and saw the outline of trees and houses. We were about four blocks away from the bricked streets of Ashland when Dad sped up to shoot the truck past the last large drift.

We felt the front tires bounce, the truck slowed, and the rear tires spun. Dad backed up and charged forward. The rear tires spun, and dug deeper into the snow and gravel.

"Dammit to hell." Dad began to get out. "Larry, you and Norman take the scoops and dig us out. Warren, keep an eye on the hogs. Trade off with Norman in a few minutes."

Dad found an old shovel in the truck. All three began to scoop snow and gravel. The truck rocked sideways from a gust of wind as the snow kept falling. I looked ahead and saw cars driving on the Ashland streets. Then I saw a snowplow coming down the street toward us.

I jumped out, ran to Dad, and pointed. "Snowplow."

We watched the snowplow turn at the corner and head away from us.

"Assholes won't help us," Larry said.

Dad told Norman to get in the truck to warm up. I took his scoop and tried. I could barely get any snow or gravel on the scoop.

I glanced up at the town, and wondered why no one helped us. We could die out here. Dad got in the truck and sent Norman out with instructions for us to shove when he drove forward. Larry grabbed our scoops and tossed them in.

We lined up behind. Dad backed up a few feet then gave it the gas. We leaned into the truck and pushed. The snow and gravel spun off the tires and hit our legs. The truck shot forward. We ran after it and jumped in. Finally, Dad pulled into the sales barn area and removed his diaper headgear.

Two workmen helped us shove the hogs into a pen. Dad backed the truck to a pile where Norman and I could scoop out the dirty straw.

"Toss snow in the truck," he told us, "clean that crap out of there."

When we finished he told Larry to take us to the cafe for a donut.

I figured that if I could get some milk down, I would be all right. A few farmers were sitting in the cafe, drinking coffee and smoking cigarettes. Patches of soft mud covered the floor. Larry gave the waitress a smile as he sat down on a stool. Norman and I sat on each side of him.

"Hey Mabel, give these boys a glass of milk and one of your donuts. Coffee for me."

When she brought our order, Larry asked, "Doing anything tonight?"

Mabel looked a little older than Larry. Her dress seemed too tight, her parts bounced around when she walked. But if our uncle liked her and liked to look at her, it was okay with us. The sugary-glazed donut forced the roughness of the trip out of my memory.

"How about you, Larry? A boy like you ever get out of Wann? Come to town, look for a little fun?"

"Just might tonight. Where can I find you?"

"Jolene and me going to that dance in Yutan if it quits snowing. Beer is cold and the polka band is hot."

Just then Dad walked in. "Sale's started. Let's go. The man says they got buyers for hogs."

Norman and I finished our milk and donut, Larry paid for them and gave Mabel a dime tip. The sales barn felt warm inside, and the donut was the best treat I had for weeks.

We sat on low, dusty bleachers and watched hogs, cows, and sheep change hands quickly. Our two pigs entered, received an offer, and then they were chased out.

Dad smiled. "Sixty dollars! Meet me in the truck. We'll go downtown and get lunch."

I wished Dad would take us home right then. Maybe we could open a Christmas catalog and pick out a present. *We were going to get one for sure*, I thought. But, lunch downtown? Another treat? What would I get? Dad pulled up in front of Hoffman's IGA and walked inside.

Through a window we watched a donut-making machine. The first time I noticed it, I stared for twenty minutes. I couldn't imagine what kind of machine could bake a donut and then roll it down to a counter where a girl sprinkled sugar on it. A magical machine, nothing in Wann came close.

"Larry, you got a date with Mabel?" Norman asked.

I stared at my brother. Twelve years old, he was getting far too interested in females as far as I was concerned. Wasn't he going to keep playing baseball and the chase 'em games we ran on the Wann roads?

"Don't know Norm. How 'bout you? You got sweet on anyone yet? Got any girlfriends?"

"Yeah. I got two at school."

Well, I'll be darned. Norman and a girl was news to me. I had watched older boys capture girls and take them down into the storm cellar. I wondered why but didn't care.

A thought came to me. "Larry, what about Patty Newberry? I think she's cute. I saw you talking to her on the swing behind the store."

Larry looked out his window and didn't answer for a while.

"Yeah, she's really cute. But she wouldn't give me a kiss when I asked her."

Norman and I stared at each other.

Dad walked up with a grocery sack and his friend, Bremis. Something was up; I could tell by the way Dad was smiling.

"Here boys," he said, "take two slices of bread. Put a slice of liverwurst between them. Then pass around the bottle of milk."

Liverwurst? I hated liverwurst. Hated it totally, even worst than cheese and mincemeat pie. I ate two slices of bread without any meat. At least I had a treasure in my belly—that glazed donut.

"Larry, take this jar. Bremis gave us homemade grape wine. You know. A little holiday cheer for Christmas."

All of us drank from the glass milk bottle. I was hoping we would head for home. Dad had enough money now; maybe we could get a six-dollar present this year.

"Larry, Bremis says they're getting up a poker game in Memphis if the roads are open. What do you say, want to go? We'll stop at the filling station first."

"Not much on my mind today. But all I got is a few halves and quarters."

Damn, will we ever get home? What if dad loses our Christmas money?

Dad pulled the truck into the Texaco station. "Jake, five dollars regular."

"Here Larry, take five for helping. Give this ten to dad for last month's rent. Tell him I'll catch him later for this month's."

At school I practiced math in my head. I started to add things up as we waited. Probably two for lunch, five for gas, that's seven, five to Larry, up to twelve, and ten for rent. Twenty-two dollars from sixty. That's harder. I think he has thirty-eight or forty-eight, still enough for Christmas presents.

Memphis sat eight miles northwest of Ashland, in a different direction than Wann. The storm let up, the wind died down, and the snow quit. The snow on the road billowed up around the truck.

Memphis was larger than Wann but was on the downswing also. It had store buildings on one side of the downtown road. Most of the buildings looked boarded up because of the storm.

Dad parked in front of a tall wooden building; we trooped in. Off to one side sat a candy and cigarette counter, half full, no one behind it. Next was a pool table, then a potbelly stove, and finally a poker table.

Dad told us, "Leave your jackets on 'till it warms up."

He walked to the stove where Bremis was tossing in pieces of wood. Norman and I stood as close to the stove as we could maneuver. When clouds of smoke began to billow out, we moved away, back toward the pool table.

After a couple more men had walked in, Dad told us to practice our pool playing, didn't cost anything today. Just don't cut any rips in the green felt, he warned. We took off our jackets, grabbed pool sticks, and began to smack red balls around the table. I had to stand on my tiptoes at times. The building warmed, and the smoke hung at the top of the ceiling.

We heard the nervous chatter as the poker game began. We pretended we were big-shot snooker players. But in the back of my mind I had a worry. If Dad lost that hog money, he would catch hell when we got home. There would be a serious fight and that always scared me. Probably no Christmas presents.

We glanced up as a man and his son walked in the door. The boy pulled his dad over to the candy counter and pointed. The man tossed a dime on the counter, and the boy pulled out the biggest Babe Ruth candy bar I had ever seen. Rich people! *No one should be able to do that in front of us*, I thought.

The man joined the poker game. Norman and I stared at the little rich kid. Then he wanted to play pool. *No way*, I thought, but Norman had a kinder heart. So here's what the little fart did; he placed his half-eaten Babe Ruth bar on the edge of the table and left it.

I swear each time I walked by that bar my mouth watered. The nerve of that kid! After a while, he quit playing, left his candy bar, and went to stand by his dad. I knew better than to pick up someone else's food and eat it. I could hardly bear the agony of being tempted. Didn't bother Norman, he was always stronger than I was.

Larry came over to play pool with us. "They busted me," was all he said.

We heard the gamblers talk and the ping of silver coins as they hit the wooden table. Then we heard Dad yell, "Dammit!"

We looked as he slammed his fist down on the table. We laid our pool sticks down and hustled for our jackets. A minute later Dad yelled out, "Hot damn!"

We waited as he stuffed dollars bills in his pocket and then headed for the door. We followed him out.

"Lost twenty on one hand. Won back fifteen on the last."

I wondered how much of those sixty dollars he still had. It was quiet as he drove out of Memphis. Dad and Larry didn't joke around as they had been doing. A mile out of Memphis the truck reached a Y in the road. Dad coasted past a snow covered stop sign and then Larry yelled, "Patrolman!"

As Dad stomped down on the foot feed, Norman and I turned to look out the back window. A farm sat across from the Y. We could see a black and white state patrol car with two red lights on top. We watched the patrolman open up his door, and then as our truck picked up speed, the snow billowed up behind us and we couldn't see anything.

Fright took hold of me as Dad asked Larry, "Who lives in that farm around this curve?"

"I think it's the Kolbs."

Dad gunned it around a long curve and then we saw a farmhouse with a couple of outbuildings off the right side of the road. When Dad slammed on the brakes, the truck slid back and forth, and Norman and I smashed into the side boards.

Dad whipped the truck around the farmhouse and shut off the lights and engine. A minute or two later we watched the patrol car's red lights race past the farm and on down the road. Dad and Larry began to laugh; I thought Dad was actually giggling.

We sat there for ten minutes. Then Dad started the truck, spun the tires, and drove out of the yard. He turned back toward Memphis and drove as fast as he could on the snow-packed roads. We had to take the long way home. When we drove into Wann, heavy storm clouds had darkened the village.

We stopped at the bank building. Dad handed Norman the grocery sack with a half loaf of bread and a few slices of liverwurst.

"Give this to your mom. Tell her I'm taking the truck over to Sam's for a short visit."

When we walked in our building, Mom came to greet us.

"Did you boys stay warm? Have any supper yet? I can fry a slice of minced ham for you, that's all we have."

After we had taken off our winter clothes, Norman handed her the grocery sack. She looked inside and then at us.

"Where's your father? Didn't he buy the groceries I asked for?"

Just then I remembered Mom telling Dad to buy groceries in town. Norman told her, "Guess not."

She took a deep breath while we stood there; I worried that maybe something was our fault.

"Okay," she said, "start from the beginning. Did he get the hogs to the sales barn and sell them?"

"Yep."

"How much did they bring?"

"Sixty dollars," I said, since I had been doing the math.

"Okay boys. Now, if he had sixty dollars, what happened to it? He didn't gamble, did he?"

I said nothing. Norman hesitated, and then replied, "He took us to Memphis for about an hour. There was a poker game."

I figured that since we're now spilling the beans, I blurted out, "Dad outran a patrolman and ditched him."

Mom drew in a breath and said, "Boys, eat some supper. Then you're going to bed early."

Norman and I ate, unfolded our couch, and got in bed. Mom turned most of the lights out and sat down to wait. I worried that there would be a fight. I could tell Norman was staying awake also. Did Dad have enough money for Christmas presents?

Finally, we heard Dad open the door and walk in. It surprised me that Mom remained so calm.

"Boys said the hogs brought sixty dollars."

"Yep."

"Where is it?"

"Had expenses—gas, paid Larry, paid rent."

"Okay. Where's the groceries? Where's the money for the boy's Christmas presents?"

"Forgot groceries. Had bad luck at poker. Here's all I have left."

"Fifteen dollars?"

"Yep."

They moved into the kitchen, so I strained to hear. I heard Mom say something about five dollars each and the Ashland Variety store.

Dad said, "Larry and me going to town on Monday. Bremis said the locker is hiring guys to unload turkeys and ducks. Pay ninety cents an hour. But you sure those boys need another damn toy? Seems like they break them up as fast as they get them."

"Give me the dollars. Maybe you won't get a present but they will. If you'd stop that damn gambling and get a job, we'd have enough to eat and better clothes for them."

"Hey, you listen to what I said? I'll work every day I can. Might need two days to earn grocery money. You'll get it. Going to ask about that bookkeeping job at the elevator."

They talked some more, but I was too excited to listen. I was happy to be on the couch and warm. Mom had piled a few old blankets on us. The last waves of heat from the oil stove reached us.

At last, I could sort out my thoughts. We trucked the hogs to Ashland and sold them. I got a donut and lunch in town. Dad had outrun a patrolman. The main thing was Mom made sure we would get one present. But what present would she get for me at that store? I tried to recall the toy section, was there anything I liked?

My head was full of grateful thoughts. I could imagine rich kids in town pouting because they weren't getting all the toys and games they wanted. A feeling welled up inside of me that I didn't recognize. I was so glad I could cry. I did, just a few happy tears.

CHAPTER SEVENTEEN

December, 1989

Late December, 1989, I traveled the last time to see Dad.

I drove to Lincoln and walked up the stairs to the third level. As I walked through the waiting room, movement in the corner caught my eye. Dad was sitting in his wheelchair, his back to me.

I sat down on a bench to watch him. He had a newspaper and a phone book in his lap. He tried to push quarters into a telephone. Finally, he got through to Kenny. He told Ken to place a two-dollar bet for him.

I wasn't surprised or bothered. Maybe if this were the highlight of his day, so be it. He had something to look forward to. I went over and tapped his shoulder, then pushed him back to his room where we talked.

His face looked healthier than when I first brought him to the home. *Almost as if he were being prepared for something*, I thought.

"Dad, why don't you tell me about the fight you had with a farmer? I can't remember what it was about."

He told me parts about the fight, but his memory slipped and he talked about attending business school in Lincoln. He talked about bumming a freight to Kansas City where he begged for work in exchange for food. He talked about having his expensive watch stolen in Florida. He told me how someone robbed him of the Lincoln racetrack program franchise.

A nurse interrupted to pour a mixture down his stomach tube. When I told him goodbye, I took a close look at him. *Not looking too terrible, but still trying to bet the ponies*, I thought.

A week later, on January 31, 1990, the phone rang at five in the morning. Kenny said Dad passed away during the night. A certificate listed causes as collapsed lungs, pneumonia, and Parkinson's. I met with Kenny and Mickey the next day to plan arrangements.

A selfish thought entered my mind. No longer would I have to make the trip and become depressed. Then a better thought entered—no longer is Dad hooked up to tubes.

I thought that by moving away to college, I had escaped him. I purged my harsh thoughts toward him as I grew. I think he also changed in the way he accepted the life style I headed toward, different from his.

1953

Late August approached with the state fair, Grandpa's watermelon stand, and the gathering of school supplies. Several events took place before school began.

Voices forced me awake one night. I raised my head into the glare of the light bulb. Crusty matter had almost pinned my eyelids together. As I dug pieces of sand out of my eyes, I heard Mom and Dad.

"It's midnight. How long you been driving?"

Norman crawled off of our fold-out couch. From the back of our building, Mickey and Kenny stumbled to the center table and looked at Dad.

"What did you bring us?" Norman asked.

"Do any good at the races?" Mom demanded.

I moved to the table to eat a store-bought sugar cookie with one hand. With my other hand, I tugged up my shorts.

"Have some cookies, boys." Then to Mom, "Quit pissing and moaning about the horse races."

I could tell by the way Dad talked that he had lost money. With sugar crumbs nestled between my teeth, I climbed back onto the couch. I knew that the next day we would have to get used to having Dad being in charge.

The next morning he played his new record. "If I Knew You Were Comin', I'd Have Baked A Cake."

"Boys, I may have brought home some bad luck, but I've got a good tune."

Norman whispered to me, "I don't know whether to fart or go blind."

He's getting funnier than Dad, I thought.

Dad played his record repeatedly. He made us sing along until we knew it. Then when his relatives stopped in, we had to perform it. Most of them thought it was hilarious. Before dinner we faced the usual problem of food and money shortages.

"Norman and Warren, pull up the edge of the linoleum," Dad ordered.

The linoleum was cracked and broken. So it was easy to raise one thin edge. Dad moved two chairs and slid the table out of his way.

"Hold it up. I'm looking for coins." He lowered himself to his hands and knees and came up with two dimes and three pennies.

"I'm going to the store."

We watched Dad walk to the general store. I wished I had found one of those dimes. A large candy bar and a bottle of Royal Crown Cola would have been mine. When Dad returned, the family sat down to eat. He placed a large jar of pickled pigs' feet on the table.

"Here," he said, "this meat has vitamins in it."

He spooned a helping onto each of our plates. A briny smell took away most of my appetite. I used my fork to scrape the jelly-like gobs from the small white bones. They looked like the loose snot Grandpa shot from his nose to the ground. I forked a piece of meat and bone and resorted to a trick I had learned. When Dad wasn't watching I gulped the pigs' feet and then pinched my nostrils together.

"Chew the bones," he said, "they're soft enough."

He enjoyed the meal. We had learned if we didn't eat what was before us; it was a long haul to suppertime. We had eaten pigs' feet before, but I preferred fried chicken feet. Mom fixed Elaine a bowl of chicken noodle soup, none of us complained. She was everyone's favorite and we accepted that.

It was a sunny Saturday, so Norman and I took our Red Ryder BB guns over to the schoolyard. We shot at sparrows and blackbirds, never doves or robins, but we didn't know why.

We walked around the schoolyard which seemed so big to me. Whenever possible we played football or baseball on the largest playing field. Around the school building, I could see the usual—swings, teeter-totters, a cement cave, two outhouses, a merry-go-round, and a red water pump. The building, built of gray cement blocks, had a white bell tower on top. Inside there were three rooms: a little room for grades one to four, a bigger room for grades five to eight, and a recreation room.

After an hour, we walked back to our house. Grandpa was cussing, and Grandma was crying. Something about their school bus route.

Most of the kids attending the school arrived from the

surrounding farms on the "school buses." Dessie Wilson drove her large station wagon to the south and west of Wann to pick up kids. Grandpa and Grandma drove their panel truck to haul the kids from the north and east. They were paid twenty dollars a month.

Farmer Milo Nast was on the local school board, and he developed a gripe against our grandparents. We didn't know why. Some people said this Nast character was a German. Grandma said that if Nast got his hands on a dollar bill, it was a prisoner for life.

The school board president had called Grandpa to tell him the news. For the next school year, Kaiser, a good friend of Nast, would take over the north route. When Norman and I walked in, our grandparents were telling Dad of the injustice done to them.

"We can't make it without that check." Grandma cried, dabbing her eyes with her hankie.

Grandpa was smoking one Camel cigarette after another. The glum scene forced us to sit down quietly. When the conversation became hushed, Mom spoke to us, "You boys go outside now."

We sat down on the cement slab. Norman edged over to the screen door to listen.

"Dad's going to beat up Nast." Norman reported after five minutes. "He and Grandpa are going to trick Nast to come to the general store. Then Dad will fight him."

Just then Mom stepped out. "Boys, go over to the playground. Stay there 'til I call you home."

Norman and I raced our bikes one block south, scattering red chickens and white chickens. Mick and Ken followed on their bikes. We stopped at the school's driveway. Then we looked back to see if anyone was scouting us.

"Hurry up. We'll sneak around." Norman encouraged us.

He led us one more block south to where our abandoned clapboard shanty stood. Norman turned west, so we followed him to the railroad tracks. Turning back north, we got off our bikes behind the elevator.

"Dad's going to call Nast and disguise his voice." Norman explained. "Dad's going to tell him to come to Wann. Meet in front of the store. Going to tell Nast that he's Newberry, the grocer."

A sick feeling stirred my gut as we snuck around the elevator so we could watch the store. The afternoon quietness was unsettling. No cars moved, no dogs barked, no roosters crowed.

"Quiet," Norman commanded as we heard a car coming toward the store.

Grandpa's light green '50 Chevy rolled slowly into view; we saw Dad in the passenger seat. The car coasted to a stop in front of the store which was now closed.

As the noise of the car faded, I glanced at the store and the Fire Chief rust-red gas pump in the front. The store's door and windows looked like a face to me, a face with a grim smile.

Another "Shhh," from Norman as he pointed down the road again. It was Nast's black '48 Ford. The enemy had arrived.

As Nast's car rolled to a stop next to Grandpa's, Dad jumped out and yanked open the door of the Ford. I had never seen him move so fast. As Nast came out and up, Dad struck him in the chest with his right fist. Nast didn't have a chance, trapped between the open door and his car seat. When Dad swung his left fist into Nast's belly, Nast crumbled down the side of his car until he was sitting on the road. I didn't want to watch, but I couldn't take my eyes off.

Dad moved in as Nast struggled to get up. Norman rose up and pounded his fist into his hand as we watched Nast kick Dad in his injured knee. Dad had told us because of that knee, the Army rejected him in 1942.

Dad limped backward and Nast slugged him in the face, twisting his head around. Dad lowered his shoulder and blasted into Nast, driving him back into the side of the Ford.

Nast received two fists pounded into his gut to finish him. We couldn't hear if Dad said anything to Nast as he reached down and lifted him up. Then he bounced Nast against the side of his car and pushed him back into the Ford. Dad limped to Grandpa's Chevy, and they drove off.

"Sit still," Norman said.

We watched as the overall clad farmer straightened himself up, started his car, and then drove out of Wann. Silently we walked our bikes back around the blocks to the schoolyard.

"What's going to happen?" I asked Norman.

"Don't know. Maybe Dad will run away."

An ache like a green apple sickness coiled my gut. "I'm going home," I said.

They followed me the last block. Quietly we parked our bikes and then Norman opened the screen door and led us in.

I saw Mom and Dad in the kitchen. Both had worried looks which I thought was unusual for Dad. He had on a white undershirt. He was shaving. I could see a red bruise on one side of his face. We quietly ate our supper that Mom had set on the table. It was cold mashed potatoes with a goulash mixture on top. A square of red Jell-O ended our meal.

"Boys, get ready for bed. Keep your mouths shut," Dad ordered.

"But it's the night we listen to Gangbusters!" I cried.

He advanced toward me and raised his voice, "I said to keep your mouth shut and go to bed. I mean it!"

There was never any arguing with him. I was disappointed as hell. Listening to the radio at night was exciting for us. But no, not tonight. Norman and I unfolded the main room couch and spread two sheets over it. We took off our blue jeans, t-shirts, and shoes and socks and then laid down. The phone rang one long and two shorts, our signal.

Dad answered. "Hello...okay....thanks."

I turned on my side to see what was happening. Dad was buttoning his white shirt.

He looked at Mom and said, "Hurry, get my suitcase. A patrol car just went toward Nast's farm."

We watched Mom go to the closet and pull out a small, cardboard-style case. Dad limped across the room and pulled clothes out of a drawer.

I relaxed my neck muscles and lowered my head. I couldn't make sense out of my mixed feelings. I knew what he did wasn't right, but at the same time, I didn't want him punished. It's hard to sleep when you're scared. Scared about what would happen to Dad, and where would groceries come from for the next few days.

Dad was gone the next morning. We ate one piece of toast covered with homemade apple butter. Then we sat in the back of Grandpa's Chevy for the trip to Ashland. Guessed Dad had asked them to take us for groceries. Most of the time we could raise as much hell as any rural kids, but we had learned there were times to be quiet.

Grandpa parked in front of Harold's Grocery. Mom, Elaine, and Grandma walked in. Grandpa lit his Camel cigarette and turned on the radio to listen as the Six Fat Dutchmen played polka music. We listened to a news report about the war in Korea.

Grandpa turned and looked at us. "Boys, I think your Uncle

Wendell is over there in that war."

I guess we were used to that situation. Our Washburn aunts and uncles would stay with our grandparents for a while, and then they would go somewhere else. I didn't know where Korea was, but I could tell Grandpa was worried.

We waited in the back seat until Mom came out carrying two brown sacks. On the seven mile trip back to Wann, Norman leaned over and whispered, "We have to build a fort when we get home."

I glanced at the front seat where the three adults were sitting. "What for?"

"Those Nast boys will come to Wann to beat us up."

When we reached home, we trooped in after Mom, trying not to show our excitement. We crowded around the table to see what food was in the sacks. A dozen eggs, a quart of milk, a box of Cream of Wheat and packages of meat. I knew we teetered on the edge between poverty and the county poor house, but for a couple of days, we would eat well.

After dinner Norman led us outside.

"Come on. We'll take the wagon to the railroad tracks. Load it with rocks for ammunition."

Just like killing animals, I found myself doing something I would rather not do.

The Nast boys would sometimes ride their horses into Wann. Then if we were playing in the yard, they would throw green apples or rocks at us until we ran into the house.

We filled our wagon with railroad rocks which had sharp edges that sparkled red and purple. We pulled and pushed the heavy wagon home.

Norman led. "Put our bikes and trikes in a line from that tree to the telephone pole. Fill in the spaces with the wagon and the scooter. Stack the rocks in piles behind them."

Norman went back to the shed and soon appeared, pulling two galvanized boilers to fill in the gaps.

"Now if those bastards show up, we'll be ready to fight them."

We sat down on the cement slab to rest. We heard the phone ring. A minute later the screen door opened and Mom appeared. She began to say something to us, but stopped when she saw our junk. She looked at our fort and then she looked at us and remembered the call.

"Our hogs got loose. They're in Myrtle Lehr's flowers. Go chase them home."

We ran to get our yardsticks. Grandpa had given Norman a real whip with a loose twist at the end. He liked to snap it down on the hogs' butts.

We located the hogs, three Spotted Polands, dirty white with dark spots on their hide. After we yelled and smacked them, we herded them down the sandy road into our lot. Norman pushed the fence post back in place. There was nothing more frustrating than trying to get a pig to go where you wanted it. It made me feel better to strike out at something, to inflict pain rather than feel it.

Dad's car was in front when we returned home. Half of it was sticking out into the road because of our rock and junk fort. I followed Norman inside and saw Dad sitting at the table with his friend, Bremis. There was a bottle of Mogan David wine between them.

Bremis seemed to be a different sort of fellow. After every drink, his tongue would quickly slide in and out of his mouth. They were laughing at some joke, but when Dad saw us, he nearly jumped out of his chair.

"Dammit, you guys get outside and clean up that mess. What the hell kind of game you playing? And haul those rocks back to the track. That's railroad property. You want us all to get arrested?"

After supper Dad told us Nast wasn't going to press charges. He said he had Bremis lined up to appear at his trial as a character witness. With the family settled down, we decided to play a game we had invented. Norman took the wagon, I took the scooter, and Mick and Ken rode their red tricycles. We went one block to the front of the store where the road widened out. The place where the fight had taken place.

We separated about five yards and then crashed our playthings into each other as hard as we could. Made a hell of a racket. Dented and scratched up everything. Sometimes we would fall and get a bruise. After five minutes of banging and crashing, Newberry the grocer, stepped out and yelled at us.

"Get the hell out of here. You're too damn noisy!"

Before we made up our bed, I heard Dad tell Mom, "I borrowed some money from Bremis. Going to Fonner Park at Grand Island for a couple of days. Feel lucky, sure to make a killing."

After the light had gone out, I had time to think about the last two days. Life for our family seemed to be on a downward spiral. We're still living in a house with no indoor plumbing. Mom has begged to move to a bigger house in Ashland. Grandma and Grandpa lost some income. Dad beat up a farmer and escaped in the night. We live in fear of getting beat up by older boys. I'm sick way too often. Now Dad is going away again.

The next morning I had to get away. I walked over to the schoolyard. In one corner, there was a soft grass area where I could lay down. I put my hands behind my head and looked up at the clear blue sky and the fluffy white clouds.

I closed my eyes and pictured a large farmhouse. Inside sat a long table, and on it there were three large platters of fried chicken. The skin was crispy brown, almost black. I could smell the greasy, frying aroma. Next to the platter were three large yellow bowls full of fluffy, mashed potatoes. Three baking bowls sat near full of light brown chicken gravy.

I pictured three loafs of fresh-baked white bread sitting next to glass butter boats full of home-churned butter with the cream still in it. Also on the table sat a bowl each of sliced red tomatoes, steaming garden green beans, and bright yellow sweet corn already off the cob.

Finally, I looked over to a sideboard and pictured one apple pie, one cheery pie with a thin crust that crisscrossed over the cherries, and one large chocolate cake covered with rich chocolate frosting, my favorite. I lay there for a while trying to get pickled pig's feet, wet poached eggs, and rings of bologna and sauerkraut out of my mind.

Later I walked home with two thoughts in mind. Maybe someday our family would sit down to a meal like that. Also, I doubted that I would ever grow up to be a fighter like Dad.

With Dad gone, we felt we could act up more. I almost made Kenny cry because I called him Tailspin Tommy too often. The only reason I did it was because I knew he would react. I thought it was his fault. When he told Mom, she gave me hell which made me feel ashamed. Once Norman rode his bike out of Wann to a friend's farm without telling Mom.

During the annual Ashland festival called the Stir-Up, there was a local talent show, still held even though the TV was getting control of people's minds. Hundreds of people attended the show at the bandstand in a small park between downtown and the Salt Creek Bridge.

Dad had quit forcing Norman and me to go along with his crazy schemes. However, he signed up Mickey and Kenny to sing in the show. Truthfully, I felt sorry for them but was happy that I didn't have to suffer with them. They sang, "I've Got a Lovely Bunch of Coconuts."

They got though it but didn't win any prize. I was glad for them when they finished. Maybe things were looking up for me if I could always be included with Norman. But I didn't feel that way if I were expected to do all the labor he did. Seemed like nothing was ever entirely white or black. There was always a shade of gray mixing up my thinking.

CHAPTER EIGHTEEN

1953

After I turned twelve, I suddenly realized something. Dad had quit whipping Norman and me. Maybe he realized it wasn't doing any good.

I could feel that Norman was drifting further from me. I wondered what would happen when he graduated from high school. It wasn't meant for me to know that when that time came we wouldn't see him very often. Then in some future years we wouldn't see him at all.

After weeks of Wann living, a memorable event would occur. Grandma loved to watch all-star wrestling on TV. Popcorn popped and hard candy to suck on, we were four happy boys.

We munched on snacks and cheered on the good guy wrestlers. We liked to watch Gorgeous George from Hollywood; he was one of the bad guys, and he put on a great show. I was amazed that he didn't even try to hide his cheating. It didn't take the Washburn clan long to choose a Midwestern champion.

Our hero was a good guy, Verne Gagne. He was pleasant looking, never cheated, and usually won. He worked hard and smart in a match. He always looked to secure a position where he could win with his favorite move, the sleeper hold. We wouldn't miss a show if we knew he was on.

One afternoon we jumped up when a car horn honked. We ran out to see Grandma getting out of her car.

"Boys, it's in the paper. Verne Gagne is going to wrestle in Ashland."

She hustled in to show Mom the paper.

Grandma said, "They'll set up a ring in the Ashland High gym. Two matches first. Then Verne will wrestle in the main event."

It was hard to believe that Aunt Jemima appeared in Wann, but this event was equally astonishing. Verne was a real man from the TV screen, and we would see him in person.

"Mark the calendar, boys. We're going." Grandma told us.

There, it's settled. Another big event to hope for, but also to worry that bad luck would jinx us.

Wouldn't you know it? The day arrived and quickly turned cloudy. After dinner the sky turned black. By three o'clock, the first warm sprinkles drove us inside. By five, the clouds opened up, and the rain fell so hard it splattered on the sandy roads. Then the call came.

"Grandpa's not driving in this rain."

I sat looking out the front window with a bitter feeling. Were we asking too much to occasionally experience joy outside of Wann? We had been memorizing the 23rd Psalm. "I shall not want" came to mind. Okay, fine, I thought, but I wished Verne had never put that ad in the paper to get our hopes up.

The rain let up so Norman put on his jacket and walked outside. I asked Mom if we could try to talk Grandpa into going. She said forget it.

The phone rang again. Mom talked softly. She hung up and grabbed her coat.

"Hurry, get your jackets. Your Grandma's going to drive us. Where's Norman?"

I grabbed my jacket and ran toward the schoolyard. The rain began to pelt down again as I saw Norman jogging home. I waved him back, and we ran around the front of our house and jumped in the back of Grandma's Chevy.

Grandma turned the headlights on as she drove like a grandma. She leaned over the steering wheel to see where to steer. Lightning splintered the dark clouds. The wipers couldn't keep the rain off the window. From the backseat, my brothers and I leaned forward to help watch.

There was a sheet of water between the ditches. Grandma drove little by little since the Chevy slid back and forth. There was no talking from the back seat, just four pairs of large eyes looking forward. Finally, the car's tires were on the smooth, water-covered brick streets of Ashland.

Grandma parked, and we ran through the rain to the high school. Mom bought our tickets, and I pushed forward to see for sure that there was a wrestling ring set up on the gym floor. We sat together, holding tight to our seats, not giving them up for anyone.

We were close enough to hear their bodies slam on the mat. I sat tense, not even booing the bad guy. Afraid he might come after me. Finally, our hero appeared in the flesh. He didn't disappoint us. I cheered right along with Mom and Grandma.

I wasn't too worried for Verne since his match went according to script. The evil guy got the upper hand at first. Toward the end of the time limit, Verne applied his sleeper hold and the fight was over.

Norman got Verne's autograph on a program. He gave it to Grandma after we reached Wann. All of us were quite satisfied on the ride home. The rain had quit, and the car didn't slide in the ditch.

1954

During the summer and fall of 1954 more significant changes happened to our family. I turned thirteen years old, Norman was fourteen and ready to go to the high school in Ashland. Dad bought a used '46 Ford, so Norman could drive to Ashland and stay after school for football and track practices.

When Dad drove into our front yard, Mom said, "Harry, isn't this the car you bought back in the forties?"

All of us trooped around the car. It could have been.

Dad said, "Don't think so. Mine was fancier."

This Ford had been fancy at one time, a two-door coupe. Now it looked beat up and had rust around the fenders. In the front was the large black hood, the steering wheel as large as a calf's feed pan, and four large balloon tires. Of course, Norman loved it. He carried water in buckets from the pump and spent a lot of time washing it.

"I'm getting a necker's knob to put on the steering wheel." Norman told me. "All the cool cats in Ashland have one."

"What's a necker's knob?"

"Later, you're too young now."

Norman received a learner's permit to drive to school and back home. He wasn't supposed to drive around Ashland. However, when a chance came to give a girl a ride, he was more than happy to risk the permit.

Whenever I rode with him, he loved to stomp on the clutch and shift gears as fast as he could. I wanted to be with him, but his reckless driving scared me.

The fun games we played around Wann abruptly ended. I could boss the two younger brothers, but I was a better follower than a leader. My heart wasn't into being the man of the house as Norman was when Dad was gone.

On the one hand, I wanted to grow older, do things my brother and younger aunt and uncle could do. But I missed being a little kid with Wann as my playground. To an outsider on a summer day, Wann would appear as a place where nothing happened.

I still maintained my reluctance to work. For the last two years, Norman had swept the hall and big room in the school. Sometimes Mom made me help him so he could finish earlier. Those nights I would get a nickel. I never thought about what would happen to the floors when he graduated from the eighth grade.

"Warren, ask if you can have the sweeping job this year."

Mom ruined my first day of school with that statement. School was fun, recess was enormous fun, and reading was exciting. I waited until the end of the school day before I reluctantly approached Mr. Lewis.

"Un, does anyone have the sweeping job?"

"Norman Stokes asked."

Outwardly, I looked dejected. Inwardly, I was celebrating.

"Mom, the Stokes boy got the job. He must have asked early."

"Okay, but with Norman gone, you have to do all the chores by yourself. Mickey and Kenny are too young. They can do the dishes."

That's fine, I thought. Let them sit in front of the used TV and the rabbit ears that Dad bought. We only had three calves anyway. And I wasn't tied to the school building each night.

I began to realize that our family's life was made up of small events. Everything moved forward on the calendar. Norman being gone affected me like a pain that wasn't physical, more emotional.

The television cheated us of our Saturday night entertainment in Ashland. We got a treat like popcorn or fudge to watch our weekly specials. *The Variety All-Star Revue* was okay, but my favorite came after that. I felt that Sid Caesar was the funniest person on TV. His show lasted an hour and a half, *The Show of Shows*. Then *Your Hit Parade* came on. I thought Snooky Lanson sang "Shrimp Boats are A'comin'" every Saturday night for a year.

By this time, Dad was spending more time as a jockey agent. That's what Mom told us to write down on the enrollment sheet when we started school. He had to be at the horse stables early to talk to the horse owners. He was the agent for two good jockeys; it was his job to get them mounts. If they finished near the front when they rode in a race, Dad would get a percentage of their earnings.

Now he was away from home more often. At times, he had more money for the family. All of us boys had BB guns and bicycles. We got new and better shoes. Most of the time we had our hair cut in an Ashland barbershop.

Nevertheless, in the afternoons, since he was at the racetrack anyway, Dad continued to gamble. When he suffered through a losing streak, the family suffered also, just as we used to. It seemed as if nothing changed except we kept growing taller.

Mom talked about moving to Ashland, to a normal house with indoor plumbing. I thought it over and figured our boyhood days of fun in Wann were over. Maybe I would like to live in Ashland if we had a better house.

When I turned thirteen, I entered the eighth grade at the Wann school. Norman was in the tenth grade at the Ashland high school and driving Mom crazy with his wild ways. He drove his car everywhere. He earned money working for area farmers in the summer.

It seemed to me that Dad never changed. He would dress and leave. Sometimes he came home with money, sometimes not. His latest record was "Your Cheatin' Heart" by Hank Williams. I didn't much care for Hank. Guess he was some sort of legend or something.

Strange feelings inside made me wonder if my baptism had taken hold. I didn't know if my actions and thoughts were sins. I decided to stop being jealous of my younger brothers. I tried to stay out of trouble for Mom's sake. But Norman finally got me interested in girls. From that moment on, I began to speculate about them. I thought there had to be more about girls than dirty jokes.

Norman prided himself on his muscles and toughness. He called me ninety pounds of soap and guts. I noticed that Norman didn't mind if the girls he liked weren't the cutest ones. It appeared he fell for the wild ones. He told me stories, but I had a hard time imagining what actually happened.

When my buddies at the Wann school began spending more time talking about girls, I asked no questions. I didn't want to appear dumber than a stump. I was afraid to show my ignorance on all the subjects which surrounded the females. I hoped Norman would educate me. It appeared that he was well-versed in this subject.

I approached him cautiously one day while we were hoeing the radishes and potatoes.

"Norm, what about those dirty jokes?"

"Whatcha talking about?"

"You know. Those jokes you and your friends tell."

He stopped his hoeing to stare at me.

"Sure, I know. Not telling you."

"Because ya don't know."

"Oh, I know all right. But you, you're too young. You're still a punk kid."

"Come on Norm. I'm thirteen, in the eighth grade. Why don't you tell me those jokes?"

"Warren, you're a crazy little fart. You better shut up about them. Hey, how did you know about those jokes?"

"Well, when you guys are sitting on the swings telling dirty jokes, I crawl through Grandpa's strawberry patch. I hide behind the bushes. You know, right behind you. I can hear pretty damn good."

"If I ever catch you there again I'll twist your arm off."

"Then I'll tell Mom you're telling dirty jokes."

"Listen kid, you tell her anything and I'll hurt you, got that? Now leave off on the questions."

"Norm?"

"Yeah, what?"

"What's that one joke about a naked girl?

He hit me hard, right at the top of my arm, brought tears to my eyes. My own brother.

Since Norman was fourteen months older than I was, when he wanted to, he could get brutal. He knew a lot about girls and their ways. I had seen him walk down a dark alley in Wann holding onto a girl's arm, but I didn't know what happened in the dark.

I heard people say that Wann was a ghost town, but I never saw any ghosts. I figured about thirty people lived here. We were able to go to town about once a month except that one time when Grandma drove us in to see live rassling in the high school gym. Norm and I were used to making up our own entertainment and adventures.

One of my favorite games was to take the trash basket out back behind our house. I would hollow out a hole in the ground and then burn the garbage in it. For entertainment I would do this: I would look through the basket for paper and cardboard boxes. Cereal boxes were the best. Then I would line them up on flat ground and pretend they were city buildings. I would put a match to the end box to see if the whole city would burn down.

One day a summer breeze blew hot ashes from my game to a straw pile in our hog pen. Wow, that was a flare up for sure. And wow, did my butt and the back of my legs flare up when Dad caught up with me after the fire was out. He didn't have time to get a belt so he broke off a tree branch. Damn, it hurt, but I figured I deserved it.

Anyway, one afternoon I was enjoying Omaha going up in flames when Norm came out to watch me.

"What the hell? You're crazy as a loon, you know that. You want to burn your hands?"

I didn't pay him no mind. One box wasn't lighting the next, so I was reaching in with my bare hands to push them together.

Just then, our gigantic white rooster went prancing by, making some crackle of a noise in his throat as he sprinted out onto the road. We saw three white hens two-stepping on the road toward our house. They were making a cackling racket to beat the band.

"Come on," Norm said, "let's go watch the action."

The hens, when they saw our he-man of a rooster running toward them, turned around, but they didn't try to escape. They squatted down in the road. Our rooster jumped on top of the nearest, grabbed her neck with his beak, and started to squirm. I'll be damned if I could figure out what's going on.

"What's going on Norm?"

Big brother laughed and said, "Those hens are whores."

"What's a whore?"

"Damn, you don't know nothing do you. Them hens is getting laid."

"Is that why they lay eggs, Norm, after they get laid?"

"Oh hell. Listen Warren, the rooster is knocking the hens up. Now, don't you ever knock up a girl. You know, get her in a family way."

"Why would I want to do that Norm?"

"Just forget it kid. Go put out your fire before you get another whipping."

See, he didn't know it. Already in my mind I'm adding to my knowledge. Some day I'll put it all together. I'm smarter than he thinks.

One late fall day Norm and I were loafing in our shed, resting from running races down the main road. He was on his back on a solid wooden box. Both his knees were up, and his hands were behind his head.

I was standing with my head out an open window, trying to catch a cool breeze on my face. Also, I was watching our five sows and one boar. Wanted to see how they did that knocking up action.

"Hey kid, want to know a secret about girls?"

I turned around to look at him. "You bet."

"Two words--candy cigarettes."

"Candy cigarettes, Norm? That's a secret? You can't smoke 'em, you have to eat them."

"Just pay attention and maybe you'll learn something. You know that chubby girl in your grade, Nelda?"

"Yeah, she's a little heavy. But I think her face is cute."

"Okay, here's the deal. Offer her two candy cigarettes. She'll pull up her sweater and let you see her boobs."

"Boobs? Guys in my grade call them boobies."

"Yeah, well some people call them the Boobsey Twins but don't worry about that. Listen, you going to buy the candy cigarettes or not?"

"I don't know Norm, I don't have a dime. I'm worried about what to do after I see her boobs. Do I say thank you?"

"You don't do nothing. Just look at 'em so you learn something about girls, that's all. Why is everything so hard for you? You stupid or something?"

I thought things over for a minute then, "Hey Norm, how do you know she'll pull up her sweater?"

Norm gave me his grin. "Oh, there's lots of things I could tell you, but right now you're a little young. Anyhow, why you so worried about girls all the time?"

"Cuz they act like they know things that I don't have a clue about."

"Listen kid, I'm getting a little worried about you. I don't want the authorities shipping you off to Boy's Town in Omaha. Why don't you learn to play baseball, leave the girls to me? I have to fight them off all the time. There's more than one who's in love with my bod."

Another game I liked to play was with my bottle cap collection. I kept them in a Quaker Oats cardboard tube. I could pick them up for free behind the store after Grandpa tossed them out into the drainage. I had more Nehi Orange and Grape caps than any others, so they became the foot soldiers. The generals were the Black Cherry and R C Cola caps; I had just a few of them, so they were the most valuable. I kept them shined.

I was moving my troops through the weeds one day when Norman showed up and tossed a shovel at me.

"Let's go kid, we got work to do. Put up your damn toys."

I gathered the caps and hid the tube in the shed, so other kids couldn't find them. Then I picked up my shovel and followed Norman. We walked past the store, over the railroad tracks, and through Grandpa's tomato patch. Finally, when Norm climbed over the barbed-wire fence I had to ask him.

"What's going on Norm?"

"We're going to the sandpits. Merv and I are digging a hole in the cliff."

We walked across a sandbur patch toward the sandpits.

"What's with the hole?"

"We're going to make a room, put some stuff in there. Like that old mattress from that see-through house."

"Then what you gonna do with that mattress?"

He always looked me over before giving me complete information, as if he were wondering if he should tell.

"Then we're going to take Carol in there."

"What for Norm, why take Carol in?"

"For practice. Now start digging. Quit asking questions."

I looked at a hole dug out of the side of a sand cliff. However, I didn't begin to dig.

"Norm, you don't mean that Carol who lives two blocks down do you?"

"That's right. Now get to work."

"I don't know about this. I like her, she has a nice smile. She doesn't act rough like the farm girls. And Norm, she always treats me real nice. I like it when she talks to me and smiles."

I walked over to the water's edge to see if I could see tadpoles. Norman didn't stop me. When I looked back, part of the cliff top had caved in. Norm sat down, gathered wet sand in a ball and threw a few at me. I could tell he wasn't trying to hit me. I was glad when we walked back home since I was sure Carol was a real nice girl. She didn't deserve any harm.

CHAPTER NINETEEN

1954

During the spring of 1954, my main interest was baseball. I picked a position in the outfield since I loved to run under and catch fly balls. Norm had his old jalopy, his learner's permit, and a spot on the Ashland American Legion baseball team. Since I had turned thirteen, Mom made him take me to see if I could make the midget team. That made him mad; he wanted to drive downtown after practice and pick up the wild ones.

The coaches said I could have a position as the center fielder. Norm didn't think I'd make the team, so he was seriously pissed.

When the annual Ashland festival arrived we played a home baseball game. The plan was that everyone could bring clothes, and then shower in the school's locker room. I had never been naked in front of anyone, so taking a shower with other guys made me nervous.

When our game ended, we trooped up to the shower room. All the guys striped off their uniform and walked around naked. Their ding-a-lings swung around, but I didn't stare at anyone. Everyone had brown chests and backs and white legs except for one kid. He worked at Linoma Beach. He was suntanned all over except for his white butt. Norman said everyone called him Antelope.

I turned my back to take off my uniform. Then I walked into the shower and let a little water trickle down on me. I hustled back to my clothes and dressed quickly. I saw everyone else putting on white jockey shorts, so I felt okay about that since that's what I wore.

The baseball season ended. The State Fair began, and we worked in Grandpa's watermelon stand. School began with Norman leaving early, and then getting home late after football practice.

After school, I would walk to Grandpa's pens to feed and water our calves. Mick and Ken sat in front of the TV and watched Howdy Doody. A new show came on out of Omaha. A man in a black mask would start the show by clasping his hands like a bird flying. We were supposed to call him The Hawk and make the sign when he did.

Mr. Alan Lewis hatched up a Christmas party that year. I had to wear a Santa suit and hand out homemade presents to our mothers. They sat on my lap, and I said, "HO, HO, HO, what do you want for Christmas?" A couple of the farm mothers had butts as large as the cottonwood trunk across the ditch.

I was so relieved when that was over; I acted up when I got home. Just happy to be free of something I had been dreading. Dad quickly put me in my place.

"Why do you think you're such a big shot? Did it feel good to have those butts sitting on your lap?"

Why did he do that? I sulked over to a corner. I wished he would go away for a month. Soon, like Norman, I'm planning to spend my time away from him. I was pissed off the rest of the night. Soon I'm going to lead my own life, without him in it. I began looking for ways in which I could get the best of him, at least mentally.

FALL, 1955

Another year of life in Wann went by. By the fall of '55, a significant change would happen to me. I would ride with Norman to the high school since I would be in the ninth grade. Dad began to gain even more control of my life than he had. I kept quiet, didn't stand up for myself as usual.

I decided I wasn't going out for football. I wasn't tough enough and full-tackle football didn't thrill me at all. One afternoon Dad caught up with me.

"You going out for football?"

I stared down at the scuffed toes of my shoes. No, no, hell no. I just wanted to kick around and look at girls.

"Guess not. Wanted to weight one hundred and twenty, but I only weight one hundred and ten." I kept my eyes down.

"You go out. Try it for a week. If you don't like it, then you can quit."

He gave me an out. Maybe I could survive for one week and then check it in. Maybe the Russians would start a war and football would be called off.

"Okay." Felt as if I had signed my death warrant.

Mom bought me a jock strap. Norman called it my nose guard. I thought he would help me adjust since he had learned many things in the last two years, mostly from older guys.

When we were in the house alone, he made me strip and showed me how to put on the jock strap. *What a stupid contraption*, I thought. Too many straps going every which way. If a football helmet hit between my legs, how was a piece of cloth going to protect my privates?

I loved playing touch football on the Wann playground. I never hit anyone. I ran and threw the ball and caught it. At the high school, I would have to put on pads and instead of playing for fun we would have to bust our butts for the coach by running, jumping, and colliding. I felt a headache coming on.

"Norm, I want to stay in Wann. I don't want to go out for football."

"Look kid, I'll give you some advice. If you're around the town girls and let a fart, just laugh about it. They will. Besides, you passed the eighth grade. After that everyone goes to high school. Guess what then? You'll learn about girls and hickies and French kissing. I'll let you drink beer some night."

The next day he showed me a kitchen cabinet where Dad kept supplies.

"Here," he said, "before you go to town splash some of Dad's Bay Rum on your cheeks and neck. Girls will go crazy over you."

"Is that what you use, Norm?"

"Nah. Us older guys use Old Spice."

He pulled out a small jar with pink gobs in it.

"This is Butch Wax. Helps your crew cut stand up in front. Girls like my haircut that way."

He gave me a lot to think about. But I wanted time to stand still. I felt the same when we moved from the shack. No more touch football or playing with bottle caps or chase 'em races around Wann. No more of the slow and carefree days of childhood living.

Mom bought me new shirts and jeans. Norm showed me how to roll up my shirt sleeves a half an inch. He taught me how to roll up the legs of my jeans exactly one inch, so I looked like the town boys. He showed me how to carry my books and tablets close to my body "cuz some jerk-off kids like to knock books out of little kids' hands." He told me "don't take any bullshit off anyone."

Football practice began one week before school. I endured and survived. I ran faster than most of the town boys, so the coach put me on the first team as a running back. One night Norman picked up two girls. They sat up front with him, so I got in the back. They cussed and laughed, and one girl lit up a cigarette.

I heard one girl ask about me, the little brother. Norman said I was okay; just a little shy and I liked to play games.

She looked at me and said, "Hey kid, you know love's an easy game to play? You ever play around with your girlfriend?"

I felt like sticking my tongue out at her.

Norm told the girl to show me her boobs. Well hell, why not, I thought. I liked the girl's smell. It was like sweet shampoo or perfume. I wasn't disappointed when she didn't perform. I felt like acting crazy, so I leaned forward and softly rubbed the skin on the back of her neck.

"Hey, stop it."

"You feel as soft as my dog."

At that comment, all three turned around and stared at me.

Norman laughed and said, "He's about ready for a little necking."

I knew I didn't hurt her, so I didn't care what they said.

Norman met an older kid a mile out of town and picked up a six-pack of Bud. Norm and the girls drank and grabbed at each other and laughed. I looked at the beer can he handed me. I thought we were supposed to be in training. One thought kept me from opening the can; Mom would probably be disappointed in me. I threw the can in the ditch on the way home.

"Good beer, huh?"

"Yeah Norm, it was okay."

"You listening Warren? Got something to tell you."

"Sure. Go ahead."

"If you want to have a good time, you have to be bad."

"I ain't never had a good time. And I don't know how to be bad."

'Couple of years you'll have your driver's license. You'll learn to pick up a girl and then go park. Older girls can teach you a few things."

"Whatever you say Norm."

At the start of school Mom scraped enough money together to pay for Norman's knuckle-buster class ring. He had it two days before he gave it to his current girlfriend. So once again, Mom cried her eyes out.

When high school classes began, I had another tough adjustment period. I was nervous in the high school building. First, I had to climb two flights of stairs which made me a little dizzy. Then there were all the kids walking down the hall, being loud, pushing and shoving. At Wann there were only five kids in my grade.

I kept my head down. Once I stared at two older girls who wore tight blouses and looked at me as they walked by, kicking out their wide skirts. One of them said, "Just another one of those Wann ploughboys." It didn't sound like a good judgment, but I was sure I was country looking. Looking down at my clodhoppers confirmed their opinion.

I found my first classroom and sat down in a desk, kept my eyes on the woman teacher. A pencil dropped on the floor next to me, so I picked it up and offered it to the owner. A girl. A female with dark brown eyes who stared at me. Then she smiled. I was dumbfounded.

Why was she looking at me? One hundred thoughts went through my mind as I stared back at her. She seemed pleasant, serious, smart, and was wearing clean clothes. A cute blouse and skirt. Was she pretty? I thought so but I had no standards to judge by. She raised her hand when the teacher called "Carol."

I tried to follow the math lesson, but my mind was on the girl. I thought if I ever got a girlfriend, it would be neat if it were her. A lot of the ninth grade football players said they had girlfriends. Right now I wouldn't know what to do with a girlfriend. I missed the Wann school, the home family, and Mom's cooking.

When the bell rang, I hesitated. I followed Carol out and watched her walk with a friend. That night I couldn't wait until the next math class. After a couple more football practices, the coaches told us to wear our blue game jerseys to school. We would ride the bus to Wahoo to play their team.

After practice, Roger took me aside, "Hey buddy, my girlfriend says there's a ninth-grade girl asking about you. She likes you."

Not often in my past did I feel stress like this. I tried to keep up with the classes, I was worried about the Wahoo game, would they beat us up, and now some girl was talking about me.

I hated wearing that jersey to school. I was so thin the jersey hung down off my shoulders. As usual I hesitated at the end of math class. I noticed Carol didn't walk out.

She faced me and said, "Good luck at your game."

I blurted out, "Are you going?"

She nodded her head, smiled, then walked out. She wished me luck. Wow, was I fired up. The problem was I didn't have a game plan as we did in football. I didn't know what my next move should be. Sure, I wanted to be older and enjoy the benefits that came with it. I had no idea about the multitude of complications that would wallop me in the face. Why couldn't Norman and I stay ten years old and enjoy days and days of Wann playing?

Dismissed from school early, the team filed out of the study hall. As we walked out, the other kids clapped. I hoped they looked at Roger and the town hero football players. We suited up in our locker room and then boarded a yellow school bus.

I worried that I might vomit on the bus. I worried that we would get beat. I was afraid that I would screw up in the game. It seemed that most of my life I had been scared.

When the bus stopped at the Wahoo football field, there was no organization. Roger and a few others put on their helmets and ran down to the other end of the field. I got off the bus, one of the last, and began to walk with Dude Vosler.

I heard some chanting and noticed the visitor bleachers. A few ninth grade girls had declared themselves cheerleaders. They wore similar blue skirts and white sweaters. Other ninth grade girls sat in the bleachers. The cheerleaders bounced up and down and tried to lead the singing of the school song.

"Blue and white, blue and white, you're the colors of delight."

Suddenly I felt awkward. Our black, high-top football shoes featured one inch cleats. We had a padded girdle wrapped around our hips. At least my jersey fit over my shoulder pads. My fear was I would start to jog past them, and then somehow trip and fall on my face. I decided to keep walking. I did leave my helmet off, so the girls could see my face. Where that notion came from I had no idea.

As we approached the bleachers, I noticed Carol. Oh man, the tension and stress. Why didn't the coaches show us a bathroom when we arrived?

Then hell, hell, hell and damn, damn, damn. I saw him. Dad was sitting at the top of the bleacher. He was wearing his suit and hat. Worse yet, as we walked in front of the bleacher, he got up and hustled down. I began to walk faster. Dammit, this was my world. My team and friends. I wanted him to stay totally away from my activities.

He grabbed my arm. Right at the end of the bleacher. Right in front of Carol. The cheerleaders became quiet. Dammit, I had had enough. I didn't look at him. I jerked my arm away and moved out into the field.

I heard his command to me, "Get your helmet on. Get down there with the rest of the team."

Did he have to do that? I mean, right in front of the girls. In front of Carol? My fears left. In my mind, I saw red and black thunderclouds. I was so pissed at him. As far as I was concerned that was his last chance. I would stop buckling down to him. I wouldn't talk to him unless he asked me a direct question.

From now on, when I came home from practice I would eat supper quickly. If he were there, I would go outside. Avoid Dad at all times. Never talk if the family rode in his car. Never give him the satisfaction of having to stop to let me puke.

From that day, my mind became determined against him. Thought that when I graduated from high school I would join the service. He could keep on gambling and bullshitting all he wanted. I wanted no part of it. I thought it was about time I experienced more freedom. I didn't know yet what my own way of living would be, but certainly different from his. I was still seeing red when the kickoff floated down to me. I fumbled it and cussed myself. We won the game.

Too embarrassed to look at Carol or even talk to her, I kept to myself the remainder of the school year. Said hi to her once or twice. Some upperclassman claimed her for a girlfriend. I didn't care. There was less pressure on me anyway. Girls were okay, their smiles were special to me, but I figured I was a country mile from having a girlfriend. I was too shy, had a few embarrassing zits, no car, and less money than a fool.

CHAPTER TWENTY

FALL 1955

One October night during supper, Mom said to me, "After football practice tomorrow, walk up the hill on Boyd Street. We rented a house."

I put my fork down. It was finally going to happen. But like the time I had to beg my grandparents for food, mixed emotions struggled within me.

"You mean we aren't going to live here anymore?"

"That's right. The house in Ashland has two bathrooms and an upstairs. You and Norman get your own room."

That fantastic news didn't register. Ripped away from the familiar Wann surroundings brought change that I didn't think I could handle.

"We're not going to live in Wann anymore?"

"Nope, aren't you glad?"

I didn't want to spoil her happiness, but I felt a tearing apart in my heart.

"What about Grandma and Grandpa? Are they moving to Ashland too?"

"I think they'll live here for a while at least. We're borrowing their truck to move."

"What about Thanksgiving and Christmas? That's not going to end is it?"

"Of course not. We'll drive to Wann."

Norman was happy. Now he could run around Ashland all he wanted. He informed me that our house was close enough to the school that I could walk every day.

After supper, I stepped out into darkness and walked the block to the school grounds. Eight years I had spent in that building. I thought about Miss Barta. In my mind, she was a pretty, young lady. I would love to see her again even if she hadn't taught me the last four grades. I remembered Mr. Alan Lewis being an outstanding teacher. He kept me after school twice, but I deserved it.

I walked until I was in the middle of the playing field. The fall air felt crisp and clean as I inhaled it with deep breaths.

My brothers and I had played football and baseball here for so many days and months, even years. Thinking back, wasn't life simple then? I wished now I hadn't been so cranky. What were a few diseases and small food rations compared to the hours of no-worry games and homemade entertainment?

I realized that there would be no substitute for Wann mixers and shivarees and the Puddle Jumper and Aunt Jemima and black walnut fudge. We survived and endured. I guessed that was the most valuable aspect of our family life.

I thought of high school and of Norman drifting away from me and from the family. Sure, we were isolated in remote Wann, but we were safe. Ashland seemed strange in too many ways.

I walked back and stopped behind our building. Probably the last time I would see the shed which used to be an excellent fort for us. And the pig pen, the garden, the outhouse, the chicken sheds. Maybe now we wouldn't have to take care of Dad's cows and pigs.

With a heavy heart, I said goodbye to Jigger. We had buried him in a corner of the garden after we found him in a ditch a half mile from Wann. Guess a car had hit him. Probably one of the Nast family did it out of spite.

I sat on the shed's step and looked at our brick building. After a while, I wiped away a few tears. I recalled the last fun time the Washburn's enjoyed. Lots of relatives were visiting at Grandma's. I think it was her birthday. All of us boys sat at the kitchen table and visited with cousins.

Grandma gave each of us a slice of minced ham between two slices of homemade bread. Also, we could have a cup of hot coffee with real cream if we wanted.

I recalled the strong, black coffee, the solid brown cup, and then the blond color of the drink after I stirred in the cream. I thought the sandwich and the coffee was an enjoyable enough life for all of us, a happy family time. I tried to force those memories into my mind since times were changing.

I lay in bed that night with a heartache. I stared for a long time at our main room. The table, the stove, and the refrigerator which replaced the ice box. Then I thought of the family life we had experienced inside those brick walls. Not only were we leaving Jigger behind, it seemed as if the move would steal all our past. I felt like crying my heart out. Finally, I glanced at the large front window and watched the swaying cottonwood leaves. *I'm no longer scared of looking out*, I thought.

All the evidence we had was black and white photos showing four boys lined up in birth order and growing taller. Most of the pictures showed the front of the brick building. Once we wore new T-shirts with western scenes and cheap slacks, our Sunday school outfit. Then with bib overalls, which were cut off at the knees, kinda dorky looking.

Next, a picture with blue jeans, denim jackets, and cowboy hats, all the same. Finally, all of us holding ropes hooked onto the halter of "our" calf. I vowed to never forget the Wann boom and bust times.

Finally, I thought about Norman. I had benefitted so much from him always leading the way. Guess my folks had brought him up to look after me. So it was all gain for me, but what had I ever done for him.

I couldn't understand why he was leading an independent lifestyle that didn't include me. Seemed as if it happened when I wasn't looking. Scared about my loneliness, I drifted towards troubled sleep.

After practice the next day, I walked up the hill on Boyd Street with Roger. He lived nine blocks up; our house was ten blocks. He pointed to it and said let's walk to school tomorrow. I saw Dad's Chevy parked near a white and green house, so I walked in the door.

Mom had a bigger kitchen. We ate at our same table in a regular dining room. Connected to it was a TV room with our couch.

"Go upstairs and look in your room," Mom told me.

Dad had bought a bed for Norman and me. Norman was in the room, sorting out his clothes. I saw Mickey and Kenny in another room. Elaine got her own room. Down the hall was the indoor bathroom. I looked in at the tub, stool, and washbasin. Yep, we had a real upstairs with a flush stool. Since I threw so much trash down it, it had to be repaired after one week. I thought there was a large pipe under the stool.

After football season, I played some basketball. But it wasn't fun. You had to wear a uniform, everyone was too serious, and the guys in the upper grades took pleasure in picking on young guys since it was tradition.

My grades in the ninth grade weren't as good as my Wann grades. Roger showed me how they played at night in Ashland. For me, however, there were too many streets, trees, houses, cars, and people. Town girls didn't run away from boys. They invited boys to parties at their houses. Then they wanted to play post office or spin the bottle.

I watched boys and girls kiss at one party. It looked like fun. But when a short girl sat down on my lap while I was drinking a free Seven-Up and eating Fritos, I didn't know what to do. Her butt hurt my skinny legs. I remembered Dad's saying about having lead in your pencil. That was my thought, but I didn't know how to write or who to. But her smile lit me up.

I asked Norman about it, but he shook his sleepy-looking head.

"Hey, you know Stephanie Larson don't you? Picked her up last night outside the snooker hall. Went for a ride. Drove out to a field and parked behind a haystack."

He glanced downstairs to make sure Mom wasn't coming up.

"Boy, some girls put up a good fight, but they really love it."

All this time I'm thinking. Maybe I can learn how to get along with the girls, especially the cute ones from Ashland.

I whispered, "Norm, what did you do? Did you kiss her?"

He looked at me as if I were joking.

Like Norman, my new friends talked about girls, especially Roger. I couldn't help but think about them. At the end of school one cute girl came into my vision. She was a year older than me, and a grade ahead. However, whenever we were in a group, I thought she looked at me as if she were interested. How could that be? No way does a poor country boy deserve a gift from heaven.

One Saturday night, Norman let me cruise the streets with him. He was always on the lookout so suddenly he said, "Jump out and walk home. Think I can pick one up."

It was getting late, so I went to bed. I thought about the last song on Norman's radio, "Secret Love" by Doris Day. Why can't I have a secret love? That older girl? Dreaming is free and easy, and if no one knows then I can't be teased.

The next thing I knew the cute girl was kissing me, I was out of my head and kissing her, and then she was shaking my arm and whispering something. I opened my eyes, there was Norman, saying he needed help with his car. He said to get dressed and come outside.

Mud and weeds covered the front passenger side of his car.

Norman handed me a towel and told me to help clean it before the folks saw it. He hoped there wasn't a dent in the front fender.

"Picked up a young one. She's wild as a two dollar bill. Drove out towards Wann. Reached over to her with one hand."

He walked around the car, so I followed him.

"Wasn't watching. Buried it down in a ditch. Got a hold of Dude Vosler, his tractor pulled me out. Stay away from that girl. She jinxed me."

That's the answer, I thought. No matter what happened, our upbringing taught us to assign chance and luck when something good occurred. If something bad took place, we needed to look around to see where the jinx came from. Dad had taught us well.

School ended in May. Same as when we lived in Wann, we attended Decoration Day at the Ashland cemetery, but townsfolk called it Memorial Day. There was a short parade and then a ceremony. Norman went to work at Harold's Grocery, and we played on the town's baseball teams.

Dad was in and out, doing his normal business. I thought he finally realized I wanted left alone. One summer day when I was reading a book in my room, Mom came upstairs.

"Why don't you go with your dad to the races today? He wants you to."

I turned away from her and stared out the window at nothing. I thought, *why should I have to? This is the moment I stand up to him. I'll hate myself forever if I cave in to him.* For once I was honest with her. "I hate the races."

She stood there for a minute. I stared at the Bryant house across the street.

"Well, it's just one time. He needs someone to buy a program or get him a drink. He's older now and likes to sit."

No, I'm done with races. He can get someone else. I want some freedom. He can't boss me around all my life.

"I don't want to go. Don't see why I should have to."

Mom went downstairs and soon called for dinner. We ate early so Dad could make the first race. I brooded during the meal and didn't say anything. Finally, Dad got my attention.

"Hey, come with me today. Think I can hit the Daily Double. I'll put two dollars on it for you. Want to hit a lick, don't you?"

Damn, why can't I stand up to him? Why can't he leave me alone?

I didn't look at him. Forcefully, I stirred the butter beans on my plate as if they were pigs I was trying to round up. Just then the phone rang. Mom said it was for me. It was Gene, the pitcher on our baseball team. He said a few guys were getting together this afternoon at the diamond to play pickup. I said I'd be there.

"Got ball practice at three. Can't go to the races. Don't want to lose my starting position." I lied. Neither Dad nor Mom said anything. I went back upstairs to my room.

Ten minutes later, I heard the screen door slam shut. I peeked out the window to watch Dad walk to his green and white Mercury. He had his business hat on. I felt this was the beginning of my freedom. Mom probably told him what I said.

He got in his car and started it. I watched the Mercury pull away from the curb and cruise down the street. I then realized that I was beginning a different stage in my life. I turned on my radio and caught Bill Haley and the Comets singing "Rock Around the Clock."

I watched Dad's car round the corner and disappear. I may have let him down, but I wasn't going to let the team down. *I'm getting stronger against him*, I thought. I began to search for my baseball glove and cap.

Another thought came to me. If I'm not afraid of him anymore, then I shouldn't be afraid of anything or anyone. I thought I would throw myself into sports as Norman did. Maybe I would study harder and get better grades. I realized I wasn't as much scared of girls as I was mystified. Maybe I could learn the secrets behind those smiling eyes.

We attended the spring picnic at the Wann school and noticed that our first shack had been torn down. A different family lived in our brick house for a spell. Gradually, the red brick bank building, full of our family's memories, began to crumble apart, like our family.

I realized then I had been too young to grasp the value of time. I thought the family would last forever. But the wheel of time slowly turned and too late I found out I was wrong.

Another school year ended and then Norman joined the U. S. Navy causing Mom constant worries. I looked ahead to my unknown future knowing I had to face it without him.

Grandma and Grandpa continued to live in Wann for a few years.

The holiday celebrations moved to our Ashland house but weren't as well attended as they used to be.

EPILOGUE

If I look closely into a mirror, I can see the small scar I received between my eyes when Norman broke the glass. So I will carry that mark the rest of my life along with my unforgettable memories of Wann.

When Grandma Washburn reached the end of her days, Grandpa sold out his various holdings in Wann. He bought a small house in Ashland and lived there a number of years.

Dad became a door-to-door insurance salesman and was quite successful at it. After a while, he decided he could do that job and still attend the horse races in Omaha, Lincoln, and Grand Island. He had more money, and at times, he joked about his losses at the race track. Occasionally, he would own a shiny new car.

After his Navy tour, Norman attended college for a few years, married, and worked a variety of jobs. In 1975, he died in a motorcycle accident in Lincoln, age 35. How fortunate was I to have him as an older brother the first sixteen years of my life.

After high school graduation, Mickey married and eventually became one of the best jockey agents in the state of Nebraska.

After Kenny graduated, he attended college for one year. Then the U. S. Army inducted him. After six months of training, he hopped on a plane headed to Vietnam. Fortunately, a year later, he came home to the family unscarred.

Elaine graduated from high school and college and then was married.

I graduated from college, married, and then moved away from Ashland.

In 1984, Mom and Dad sold their house and moved to an apartment in Lincoln. They had lived there for six years before I drove Dad to the nursing home.

Dad's funeral was well-attended since many of the Wann and Ashland residents knew him.

The Ashland cemetery is located on a small hill west of town. Really, a peaceful area. The muffled town noise of trucks, traffic, and construction can't disturb the calm atmosphere. In the distance, tall trees block the railroad tracks and the rumble of coal trains. I glance at the gravel road south of the cemetery. I smile as a vague memory surfaces.

That road is close to town and after sundown it's dark. The licensed beginners parked their dad's car there for a little smooching with their honey buns. That is until the town cop or bushwhackers would sneak up behind them. I had my chance, but so long ago my smile quickly vanishes.

Now when I visit the cemetery, it's fitting that Mom and Dad's plots are not far from Grandma and Grandpa's. They're on the highest hill with a tall tree near. I walk down and look at my grandparents resting place first. Uncle Wendell's military marker is there since he never returned from Korea alive.

I look at my relatives' markers with their names and dates. Their faces, their actions, their lives remain animated in my mind. But now they no longer live in Wann. One single thought always comes forward. The mystery of existence is something that I will never be able to comprehend.

What's life all about? Their endless days, weeks, months, and years of living in Wann. At that time, it seemed never-ending until we moved to town and whatever simple goodness there was in family life became much more complicated. Life in Wann was free-wheeling for my brothers and me—in Ashland the consequences of our actions became more severe.

The meaning of life was never a topic of discussion in Wann. Day by day survival was the first order of business. My best thoughts were to embrace the finest of life which was the best of family times. And then hold tight to family when the unbearable strikes.

Live and let live and hope for the boom times. Pick the strawberries, sweet corn, and tomatoes, go to the horse races, play poker, and then go to Sunday school and church on Sunday. That was our set of guidelines for living. We weren't rich, but our family's life was full. It was all we had and then for reasons beyond my knowledge it ended.

I look at the stone next to Mom's. It's Norman's. The call came at midnight and then I drove three hours to the hospital. Mom and Dad were crying in a room. We three stood there crying and hugging. The next day we visited with a Lincoln police officer. All the time he was talking, I kept thinking--can't we go back to the second before the accident, stop it, do something.

Norman's funeral was difficult to attend; it busted me up. Of course, I miss him a lot. Not too often, but at times, he appears in a dream. When I awake I can remember the dream. He seems always smiling and looking remarkably healthy. He looks at me and usually smiles but I can't remember if he ever says anything.

Just because he is out of sight, doesn't mean he's out of mind. Already I know when the time comes, and I see him again, what I will say to him. "Hey Norm, it seems like such a short time since you went away."

Equally heartbreaking, the stone next to Norman's has Elaine's name on it. She was on the motorcycle that Norman was driving. They had spent the Sunday at the horse races in South Dakota with Mom and Dad. Then they had traveled back to Lincoln where they both lived. A double funeral was held with two ministers in the Ashland Christian Church. Elaine was 27 when she died.

At the end of each cemetery visit my eyes and thoughts never fail to travel the seven miles north where the Podunk of Wann still exists. Come with me as I travel that road from Ashland once again.

The intersection of the county road north of Ashland and the Wann road has never changed. As I leave Ashland, the first farm buildings on the west still stand. What used to be a low, almost worthless pasture is now a pretty lake with lake houses. The road to Wann is now straitened. The four iron bridges have been replaced with large culverts or low-rail bridges. The gravel is gone; the road oiled to within a mile of Wann.

Many small farms and cornfields along the road have disappeared. Now there is a large lumber mill and then a horse training complex which is about a quarter mile long. For racehorses is my best guess. There is a public golf course with grass greens and a snack bar a little more than a mile from Wann.

We turn directly east for a mile, across the still existing railroad tracks and we are in Wann. Very slowly I turn down the one main road, still sandy. On the east of the road Grandpa's house, chicken coops, cob and calf sheds continue living only in my memory. The fallen red barn has vanished. Now there is a low-roofed building with an assortment of vehicles and machinery. On the west, the

Wann Christian Church and fellowship hall still exist, but boarded up. The site of the Wann mixers and Aunt Jemima and Sunday school classes.

Overgrown weeds and indiscriminate thin trees have replaced Grandpa's sweet corn field and strawberry patch. I coast past the gray-stoned school house. Someone lives in it now. The storm cellar and one outhouse still remain. Oh, the tales they could tell.

I stop near the playing field which I used to think was the same size as a standard football field, 100 yards long. Now it seems to be about half that distance. Overcome with a profound feeling, I look at the field and see ghost-like boys, my brothers and myself, running and playing football and baseball. It's weird. Causes me to catch my breath. It's like a video tape which I can play whenever I desire.

Old man Everman's red chicken coops are still in place, but I see no chickens. At the end of the road, the Lehr house remains plus a pale green house where a Vosler family lived. I turn my pickup around and look to the west. Where our shanty once stood there is now a wheat field. The shivaree house remains, but other houses are missing. I coast back up to the intersection leading to the general store, the corner where the Wann bank used to exist.

A stucco house sits on that corner now. Our shed, outhouse and red pump no longer have life. However, across the road the cottonwood tree where we killed the bull snake continues to grow. Other trunks have fused with the main one, so its circumference is beyond measure.

Modern siding on the old general store has replaced the wooden siding with its peeling white paint. It's the site of Dad's fight. It's where the candy counter and soda cooler once fired the craving for sweets for my brothers and me.

I stop there and look to the south at the grey elevator. It seems to have shrunk, but that can't be. Finally I realize that, over the years, surrounding trees have almost reached the elevator's top, thereby partially hiding it. Across the tracks, the Wann sandpits of baptismal fame remain.

So once more I inhale the air of our village. This is not self-torture. The dreadful times have merged and faded. My selective memory recalls the best of our times.

Then more recollections than I can handle rush through my mind. I don't have any adverse feelings. I experience an intense longing, a desire fierce as fire fills my heart.

Oh, to run those sandy roads and trails again with my older brother and two younger ones. To play all our old games. To sit out back in the shed and shoot the breeze. To play football and baseball on the school grounds. To devour all you can eat free pancakes and Mom's fried chicken and black walnut fudge. To hunker down during the cold winter nights and play board games. To see Grandma in her kitchen and Grandpa in his fields. To look up to our aunts and uncles. To be looked after by a loving mother. Lower class may have been our life's circumstances, but damn, there were memorable times.

Before I leave the cemetery, I notice two pale leaves fluttering down near the Washburn stones. I look up at the tree where another leaf begins to float downward. I experience a strong yearning to catch it. Then I hear by brother's voice.

"Catch it Warren, get it!" Norman cries to me.

If my older brother thinks I can do something, I don't want to let him down. I run this way and that way trying to catch a floating cottonwood leaf in a bushel basket.

Made in the USA
Charleston, SC
30 January 2012